KV-034-502

As Chairperson of the National Council on Ageing and Older People, it gives me great pleasure to introduce this report, *Older People's Preferences for Employment and Retirement in Ireland.*

The Council has consistently asserted that older people are a heterogeneous group with diverse abilities, needs and preferences. This is particularly relevant when considering employment and retirement issues.

Furthermore the Council wishes to promote the social inclusion of older people and believes that the heterogeneity of this group must be accommodated through the provision of choices in relation to all aspects of their lives, including employment and retirement. The identification of what older people actually want is a first step in creating choices that accommodate diversity and promote social inclusion. Therefore the Council decided to commission this research to investigate what older people themselves want and their attitudes and experiences regarding employment and retirement.

The research provides for the first time a national representative quantitative review of the experiences and preferences of older people in relation to employment and retirement. The research allows a wide range of men and women, between the ages of 55 and 69 years from a variety of backgrounds and employment status, to offer their perspectives on work and retirement and their preferences for participation and non-participation in the labour force.

Among other things, the research demonstrates, that older people would prefer if there were more flexibility introduced into employment practices. Since 1982, the Council has proposed that there are no economic, social, gerontological or other reasons for the selection of 65 years as a fixed retirement age. Gradual and flexible retirement policies would acknowledge the diversity of older people's needs, preferences and abilities. The challenge is for policy to respond to this diversity and to provide realistic choices, so that the quality of life of older people in their 'third age' will be enhanced and that health and social gain are maximised.

On behalf of the Council, I would like to thank the authors, Dr Tony Fahey and Dr Helen Russell for their hard work and dedication in producing an excellent report. I would also like to thank members of the Council Consultative Committee who advised on the progress of the research and oversaw the preparation of the report: Mr Seamus Bannon, Ms Carol Baxter, Ms Mary Beggan, Mr Michael Browne, Mr Jim Cousins, Mr Niall Crowley, Ms Heidi Lougheed, Ms Leonie Lunny, Ms Ita Mangan, Mr Michael O' Halloran, Mr Peter Sands and Mr David Silke.

Finally, the Council would like to thank its Director Mr Bob Carroll, Research Officer Ms Sinead Quill and former Research Officer Ms Catherine Conlon who steered the project on the Council's behalf. Thanks are also due to Mr Eamonn Quinn who prepared the report for publication and to the Council's administrative staff for their assistance throughout the course of the project.

Dr Michael Loftus
Chairperson

Authors' acknowledgements

We would like to thank the staff of the National Council on Ageing and Older People (NCAOP) for their asistance and support in carrying our this work. The members of the Consultative Committee set up by the NCAOP in connection with the study also provided valuable guidance and commentary. Our appreciation goes to the Survey Unit of the Economic and Social Research Institute for the efficient conduct of the survey fieldwork and to Brenda Gannon who provided assistance with the data analysis.

Tony Fahey and Helen Russell
The Economic and Social Research Institute

Older People's Preferences for Employment and Retirement in Ireland

Tony Fahey and Helen Russell
The Economic and Social Research Institute

National Council on Ageing and Older People

Report No. 67

National Council on Ageing and Older People

22 Clanwilliam Square

Grand Canal Quay

Dublin 2

Report No.67

(c) National Council on Ageing and Older People, 2001

ISDN 1 900378-22-1

Price €10.54 £8.30

Cover image kindly provided by Sandwell Third Age Arts:
a project serving older people with mental health needs,
their carers and care workers.

For more information please contact Tel: + 44 121 553 2722

Older People's Preferences for Employment and Retirement in Ireland

Contents

Tables and Figures

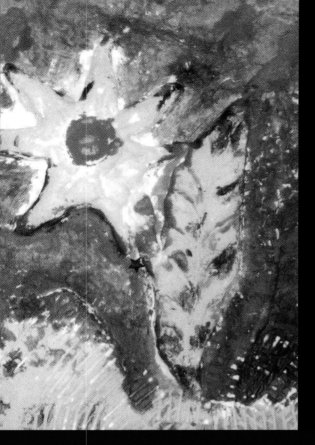

Council
Comments and
Recommendations

1

Council Comments and Recommendations

'Older People's Preferences for Employment and Retirement in Ireland'

1. Background to the study

Age has been identified as a fundamental organising principle of modern society. One of the many areas of our lives that is structured with reference to age is employment. In particular, the practice of withdrawing from the labour force, retirement, has become age related. Retirement is a socially constructed phenomenon that has more to do with the organisation of the labour market than with the preferences and abilities of older people for participation in paid employment. Despite a common belief that retirement is compulsory at 65 years of age, there is no legal age at which an Irish person must retire. In a review of retirement policies undertaken by the Council in 1982, it was pointed out that there were no economic, social, gerontological or other reasons for the selection of 65 years for fixed retirement age (*Retirement: A General Review*, 1982). Increases in life expectancy and general well-being in later years mean that people at age 65 years nowadays may be in no different a position as regards ability and willingness to work from people in other age groups. In fact, a small but significant proportion of the workforce continues to work well into their 'third age'.

For example, recent Council research (*HeSSOP*, 2001) found that 10 per cent of a sample of older people aged over 65 years (n=937) reported that they were in paid or self-employment. In addition, a significant minority (10 per cent) of those who were interviewed for the study stated that they would like to return to the workforce.

2

Part of the Council's terms of reference is to promote the health, welfare and autonomy of older people. Enabling those older people who wish to remain active in employment is, in the Council's view, one means of promoting active and healthy ageing and the social inclusion of older people. However the Council is also aware that for some people paid employment is not their preferred way of being active and participating during their 'third age'. Some look forward to the prospect of retirement and accessing their pension rights so as to pursue other opportunities and retreat from the demands of the workplace.

Recently, the issue of older Irish people's participation in the labour force has emerged onto the policy agenda due to prospective labour shortages in a booming economy. This prompted the Council to commission research on employment and retirement among older people. In contrast to the purely labour market focus that characterised other studies (eg PACEC (forthcoming)), which sought to investigate how older people could 'contribute to the boom' (Harney, 2000), the Council wished to investigate what older people themselves wanted, what their views and preferences in relation to employment and retirement were.

The following recommendations are based on the findings of the quantitative survey of a nationally representative sample of older people aged between 55 and 69 years that was conducted on behalf of the National Council on Ageing and Older People by the Economic and Social Research Institute. The recommendations highlight priorities for change that will not only facilitate older people having a real and meaningful choice in relation to the employment/retirement decision but will also promote a satisfactory work/life balance for those in their 'third age'. For example, this research has found that 37 per cent of those at work wanted to retire as soon as possible while 26 per cent of the non-employed wished to take up some form of paid work. These choices and preferences should be translatable into practice if we are aiming for a socially inclusive society. The Council has recommended that a comprehensive policy for the social inclusion of older people be developed and implemented (Loftus, 2001). It believes that the measures that are recommended in this report will help to reduce some of the barriers that exist in relation to the fulfilment of preferences and to the social inclusion of older people.

2. Older people's right to participate in the workforce

Historically older people have been considered as being a 'reserve army of labour' and in times of high unemployment, early retirement was used as a mechanism for 'making room' in the labour market for younger workers. This solution clearly favoured one generation over another (Mangan, 2001). The present study found that early retirement is common. Over two thirds of those who were retired stated that they retired before 65 years of age, with an average retirement age of approximately 59 years. The most common cause of early retirement was illness and disability. However, the second most common cause was voluntary redundancy or receipt of early retirement packages. The Council recognises that, for some, early retirement is a liberation that provides the opportunity to do other things without having the demands of the workplace and therefore it does not wish that older people be denied this right. However, **the Council recommends that older workers should be encouraged, enabled and have the right to remain in the workforce during both good and bad economic times if they so wish**. Early retirement packages should not be used as a labour market mechanism for the removal of older workers in order to accommodate the employment of their younger counterparts.

4

3. Gradual and flexible retirement

The Council has advocated revising retirement policies towards flexible or gradual retirement schemes since 1982. Such policies would both acknowledge that older people are a heterogeneous group of people with diverse abilities, skills and preferences about work and retirement and that these abilities, skills and preferences do not disappear at 65 years of age. Flexible retirement arrangements allow some freedom of choice as to the age at which the retirement pension can be drawn. Gradual retirement offers workers the option of entering retirement gradually by reducing the time actually spent at work in the final months or years before age 65 and perhaps continuing in part-time employment after that age if they so wish. Ultimately, such policies would allow older people to have a choice in relation to their participation in employment or retirement in their 'third age'.

This research found that there was a strong preference for gradual retirement (ie gradually to reduce the number of hours or days worked before stopping completely) among both older workers and workers who had retired. Approximately 70 per cent of older workers stated that they would like to retire more gradually, while nearly 50 per cent of those who had already retired stated that in retrospect, they would have liked to retire more gradually. The research also reported that there was a significant minority of respondents, between 20 and 25 per cent who would have retired at a different age had pension arrangements been more flexible. The Council recognises that it would be a complex task to alter the present pension and retirement systems so that these preferences be realised. However, **the Council recommends that these preferences for gradual and flexible retirement be given strong consideration and that future policy on pensions and retirement age be amended to accommodate their provision**.

4. Adequate pension provision

The research reported that overall, retirement is perceived as a positive state with the retired being generally satisfied with their current situation. A number of issues were found to influence attitudes towards retirement. In particular, there was found to be a significant association between income level and the level of enjoyment of life that one experienced since retirement. In addition, those who had the most positive views about retirement were from professional or managerial backgrounds, which would indicate that extra resources enhance satisfaction with retirement. This is further supported by the fact that those who strongly endorsed the view of retirement as being an opportunity to pursue other interests had the highest mean household incomes. Upon cessation of employment at whatever age chosen, it is apparent that adequate pension cover will play an important role in the quality of life that an older person will have.

Most Irish retirees are likely to receive a social welfare pension. In 2000, about 1.95 million workers contributed towards a social welfare pension. However, the value of this pension is low by international standards (Fitzgerald, 2001). The social welfare pension may be supplemented by a private occupational pension. Less than half of the workforce was covered by occupational pensions in 1995, the latest year for which figures are available, and 60 per cent of private sector and one sixth of public sector workers had no occupational pension cover (Fitzgerald, 2001). The Council endorses the view that adequate provision for retirement income in the future will require both improvements in the basic social welfare pensions and development of the private pension provision system (Hutch, 2001). **The Council recommends that the real value of social welfare pensions be increased in line with international trends and that more workers are encouraged to make private pension provisions**. The National Pensions Policy Initiative has recommended that social welfare pensions should amount to 34 per cent of gross average industrial earnings and the Council endorses this recommendation.

In addition, the Council recommends that there be active policies encouraging people to save for retirement to ensure that a sharp drop in their living standards is not experienced upon retirement. The Council recommends that a tax-free allowance be introduced for older people who work after retirement that will apply to money invested annually in a 'security fund' for use later. The Council welcomes the Pensions (Amendment) Bill 2001 which proposes to introduce a framework for Personal Retirement Savings Accounts (PRSA). The PRSA will be a low cost, easy access and long-term personal investment account designed to allow people to save for retirement in a flexible manner. It is envisaged that these PRSAs will complement the Social Welfare pension and it is hoped that the availability of such accounts will increase the level of occupational and personal pensions coverage from less than 50 per cent at present to 70 per cent of the total workforce over thirty years of age.

It is important to note the voluntary nature of this scheme in that there is neither an obligation on employees to avail of it nor is there any obligation on employers to contribute to it. **The Council recommends that any development of the private pension provision system be supported by clear institutional arrangements that will instill confidence in such schemes. The Council recommends that an information drive to convince people of the need to make sufficient retirement savings be initiated**. This is particularly important in relation to the introduction of the PRSAs.

5. The right to work and the right to pensions

The link between pensions and retirement was originally seen as removing the burden of work from older people. However, there is no necessary link between pensions and retirement and it is possible to have pensions available and to remove the exclusion from the labour market (Mangan, 2001). **The right to work and the right to pensions must co-exist and the Council recommends that an older person's right to work should not be seen as compensation for the loss or reduction of pensions.** At the moment, the pension system in Ireland discourages those with low earnings potential from becoming employed once they reach 65 years of age. The non-contributory means-tested old age pension is payable at age 65. Any earnings over a low threshold are deducted from the pension on a pound for pound basis and this acts as a disincentive to becoming employed. For those who have paid pension contributions a retirement pension is available at age 65, but any earnings above £30 per week invalidate the claim to the pension. At age 66, the contributory old age pension becomes available and there are no restrictions on earnings from employment. As a result, the current pension system pushes those with low earnings potential out of the labour market upon reaching retirement age. **The Council recommends that this anomaly in the pension system be addressed with urgency so as to facilitate those who want to remain in employment after 65 years of age to do so without being penalised financially.**

7

6. Flexible workplace practices

Health problems can prove serious impediments to an active working life. The research found this to be the case in that 31 per cent cited illness and disability as a reason for retirement. This phenomenon has important implications for health policy. It is generally acknowledged that the health of successive cohorts of older people will be affected by the extension and success of health promotion programmes targetted at younger age groups. A healthy lifestyle acquired in early adulthood may well be maintained throughout life. This would result in those reaching the age of 65 being healthier, with the real prospect of adding years to life and enabling active membership in the community for as long as possible. It is also recognised that although it may be more difficult for older people to change their behaviours of a lifetime, it is certainly possible, especially if they become partners in the health promotion process (*Adding Years to Life and Life to Years*, 1998). **The Council welcomes the *National Health Promotion Strategy* 2000-2005 and recommends that health promotion activities and preventative measures that are routinely offered to younger people be developed so that they include and are offered to older people. In particular, the Council recommends that older people be encouraged and enabled to participate in all aspects of life through targetted healthy ageing programmes which promote their health and well-being.**

In addition, there are various measures that could be adopted within the field of employment policy to alleviate some of the adverse effects of bad health on the employment practices of affected older workers. For example, more flexible working arrangements such as semi-sheltered employment for those who suffer from ill-health would be particularly relevant. More generally, the research found that among those older people who were currently working, over a quarter stated that they would retire early because work was too demanding or stressful. This also reinforces the requirement for more flexible working arrangements. The research also noted that, among those who had already retired, a quarter of the respondents either agreed or strongly agreed that they would have continued working if their employers had been more accommodating. Again, this points to the need for more flexibility both in employers' practices and in the workplace in general.

In recent years, there has been a request for more family friendly policies in the workplace to support female employees with young children in particular. Interestingly, there is some anecdotal evidence which suggests that, due to the lack of such family friendly policies, older women are increasingly taking up the role of minding their grandchildren while their sons or daughters are at work and that this precludes them from taking up employment in their own right. It is apparent that more flexible family friendly policies would not only facilitate the younger generation of workers (and especially younger women) to take up employment but would also enable some older women who would like to become employed to satisfy this preference.

The Council welcomes the Government's intention to establish a Working Group of the Department of Health and Children, the Department of Enterprise Trade and Employment, the DSCFA, the Equality Authority and relevant organisations to report on strategies for the care of older people from the labour market perspective (*Department of Social, Community and Family Affairs, 2001*).

The Council recommends that greater attention be paid to policies relating to the employment circumstances of all older workers, including those who have poor health, and that more flexibility be introduced into employment practices accordingly. The heterogeneity of the older population demands more flexible retirement arrangements.

7. Discrimination in the workplace

There is a perception that age discrimination (direct and indirect) is still quite pervasive in employment practices in Ireland and yet there is no clear understanding about how it operates in the workplace. This research highlighted that older people share this belief in the existence of discrimination. Among those in home duties who wished to become engaged in some form of paid employment, over 50 per cent stated that they were not employed because they felt that employers wanted younger workers. **The Council recommends that a dual strategy for tackling age discrimination should be adopted whereby older people are informed about their rights as workers and employers are made aware of their legal obligations in relation to discrimination in the workplace**.

Upper age limits apply in legislation relating directly to discrimination and workplace practices. As a result, older workers who are aged above these upper limits do not have the normal protections set out under the legislation. For example, the existence of the upper age limit that applies in the Employment Equality Act 1998 means that those aged over 65 years who are currently in employment have very little protection against actions of employers and are at a disadvantage compared to their younger counterparts. **The Council recommends that the upper age limits that apply in anti-discriminatory legislation such as the Employment Equality Act, 1998, the Redundancy Payments Act, 1991 and the Unfair Dismissals Act, 1993, be removed**. These upper age limits, in effect, have introduced an institutionalised form of discrimination against older people. The removal of these age limits would ensure that older people over 65 years of age would have the choice to work after the general retirement age if they so wish and that this choice would be protected by anti-discriminatory legislation.

The research found that almost a quarter of people in the combined group of persons performing home duties, the sick and less able, and the long-term unemployed stated that they would like to take up some form of paid employment. The majority of those in this group who wanted some paid employment were women in home duties who were of a younger age group (55-59) and who had been in the paid workforce for a period since they were aged 51 years. The main reason that they gave for not being in employment at the time of the interview was that they felt that there were no suitable jobs in the locality. They also felt that they did not have the right skills for paid employment and they felt that employers generally wanted to employ younger people. Discrimination in the workplace has been discussed above. Perceived lack of skills also acts as a significant impediment to the realisation of employment preferences, with over 50 per cent of this group of respondents stating that they felt that they did not have the right skills to take up paid employment.

There is general consensus that past under-provision in education has left a significant skills deficit and many older people are excluded from the workplace because they lack the necessary skills on the one hand and they lack any recognised formal qualification on the other (Costello, 2001). A disappointing finding of this research was that only approximately 9 per cent of all respondents had participated in job related training in the last twelve months while a similarly low figure had participated in some other course or some form of education in the same period. The respondents who were employed at the time of the interview were significantly more likely to have undertaken education or training than any other group.

Lifelong learning is considered as being part of the solution to overcoming barriers to employability for older people and especially those older people who have been outside the labour force for a number of years. **The Council recommends that the benefits and value of lifelong learning for older people should be publicised. The fact that it increases both their prospects of employment and their quality of life should be promoted among older people**. The Council also recommends that measures should be put in place to assist older people to ensure that they are enabled to take part in training or education programmes. Such measures should include:

- promotion of the value and benefits of training

- more information about the programmes that are available

- increased flexibility in the delivery of programmes

- greater workplace training provision

- increased targeting of programmes at vulnerable and disadvantaged groups

- increased resources allocated to training and lifelong learning to cover costs such as fees, transportation, books etc.

- the underpinning of information and knowledge acquisition by a guidance and counselling system

- the accreditation and design of training to ensure that skills remain relevant.

9. Participation in voluntary activity

One third of all respondents in the survey stated that they were involved in some sort of organised voluntary work, with those who were retired but engaged in some form of paid employment being the most likely group to be involved. It was suggested in the report that one explanation for their involvement was that they might possess the ideal combination of time and resources to contribute to voluntary activity. Whelan and Whelan (1988) carried out some analysis of voluntary activity and though they did not note the overall percentage of those involved, a comparison between their data and this research suggests that there has been an increase in voluntary activity among this age group since their study was conducted in 1988. The *Green Paper on Supporting Voluntary Activity* (1997) was launched because evidence indicated a decline in the level of volunteering in Ireland. This research clearly indicates a more optimistic view and that older people remain active in many ways well into their sixties.

The Council welcomes the proposed plans to commission a programme of research that will include quantifying the full extent of community and voluntary activity in Ireland, and its contribution to social development, to the economy and to employment. This research should provide a clearer picture of the type and scale of volunteering in this country and facilitate the identification of areas for further development.

The Council recommends that all voluntary activity be supported and that people of every age, including those in their 'third age' who already greatly contribute to this sector, be actively encouraged and facilitated to participate therein. Any barriers that currently exist in relation to becoming engaged in voluntary activity, such as age limits imposed by some insurance companies, in relation to participation, lack of funding and training programmes for volunteers should be addressed. **In addition, the enhanced quality of life benefits from lifelong learning should be promoted to ensure that it does not engender a 'work for pay' mentality to the detriment of the voluntary sector**.

10. Information provision

It is important to note that a prerequisite for an older person's ability to make an informed choice in relation to their employment and retirement practices is the availability of coherent, consistent and accessible information from a variety of sources. **The Council recommends that information about public and private pensions, taxation and benefits, lifelong learning, training and education, workers' and employers' rights and responsibilities, healthy and active ageing and recreation be made readily available (through an information strategy designed by or in consultation with Comhairle) so that older people can make an informed choice as to how they want to live in their 'third age' and beyond**.

A disappointing finding from this research was that only 19 per cent of those who were retired had taken part in a retirement preparation course. Retirement is recognised as being an important life event that can be accompanied by enormous changes in everyday life. In contrast to other life events such as bereavement, illness/disability etc., retirement is a phenomenon that can be planned for and such planning can greatly facilitate the work-to-retirement transition and thereby enhance an older person's enjoyment of their retirement years. In this regard, the Council acknowledges the valuable work currently being performed by the Retirement Planning Council of Ireland. **It also recommends that retirement planning courses be publicised and made widely available and that people are actively encouraged to participate in them and to plan for their futures**. These courses provide an important medium through which information about employment and retirement can be disseminated. Society should be organised to meet the needs of all people and should enable everyone to participate therein (Mangan, 2001). Information is vital for making informed decisions in relation to participation in society. Therefore, information is a key prerequisite to an inclusive society.

References

Costello, Ned., 2001. 'Training, Retraining and Lifelong Learning for Older Workers'. *In Conference Proceedings - Employment and Retirement among the Over 55s: Patterns, Preferences and Issues.* Dublin: National Council on Ageing and Older People.

Department of Social, Community and Family Affairs, 2001. *National Action Plan against Poverty and Social Exclusion 2001-2003*. Dublin: Stationery Office.

Department of Social Welfare, 1997. *'Supporting Voluntary Activity'* A Green Paper on the Community and Voluntary Sector and its Relationship with the State. Dublin: The Stationery Office.

Fitzgerald, E., 2001. 'The Role of Pensions in the Decision to Retire from Paid Employment'. *In Conference Proceedings - Employment and Retirement among the Over 55s: Patterns, Preferences and Issues.* Dublin: National Council on Ageing and Older People

Garavan, R., Winder, R. and McGee, H., 2001. *Health and Social Services for Older People (HeSSOP)*. Dublin: National Council on Ageing and Older People.

Harney, M.(2000) *'Let Over 55s Contribute to the Boom'* Irish Times 19/7/2000

Hutch, M., 2001. 'Pensions Policy: Maintaining Established Living Standards in Older Age'. *In Conference Proceedings - Towards a Society for All Ages.* Dublin: National Council on Ageing and Older People.

Loftus, M., 2001. 'Chairperson's Address'. *In Conference Proceedings - Towards a Society for All Ages*. Dublin: National Council on Ageing and Older People

Mangan, I., 2001. 'Older People's Access to Work, Education, Training and Information Technology: Issues for Policy'. *In Conference Proceedings - Towards a Society for All Ages*. Dublin: National Council on Ageing and Older People.

National Council for the Aged, 1982. *Retirement: A General Review. A Discussion Document*. Dublin: National Council for the Aged.

National Council on Ageing and Older People (1998). *Adding years to life and life to years*... A Health Promotion Strategy for Older People. Dublin: National Council on Ageing and Older People.

PACEC (forthcoming), *Study on Labour Participation Rates of over 55s*, Dublin: Forfás

Whelan,C.T. and Whelan,B.J. (1988).*The Transition to Retirement*. General Research Series No.138. Dublin: Economic and Social Research Institute.

14

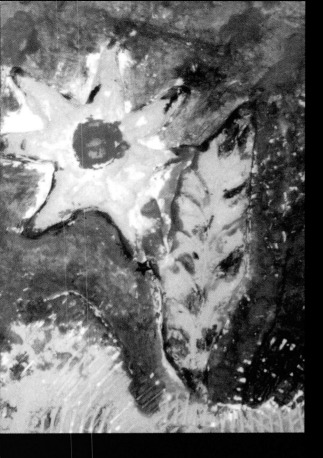

Executive
Summary

Executive Summary

Purpose of study

This report presents findings from a telephone survey of nationally representative sample of 55-69 year olds in Ireland (n=817) which was carried out in the period February - May 2001. The purpose of the survey was to examine older people's preferences, attitudes and experiences regarding work and retirement.

Work and retirement

The population aged 55-69 can be divided into three main groups – those at work (who account for over a third), the retired (who account for less than one third) and those in home duties (who account for under 30 per cent). The latter group is almost entirely female, while almost all men in this age range are either at work or retired.

Among the retired, the average age of retirement was approximately 59 and the largest group of retirements occurred between ages 55-59. Over half of the currently retired had thus retired early. Illness or disability was the most common reason for early retirement (accounting for almost one third of the early retired) and voluntary redundancy or early retirement packages were the second most common reason (20 per cent of early retired). There was little consistent variance in the incidence of early retirement by educational or occupational level; the relationship was different for actual and planned retirement.

Among those still at work, only a minority (approximately one in four) had planned to retire early. One third did not know when they would retire and 29 per cent planned to retire at age 65.

Generally speaking, late retirement was exceptional both in actuality among the currently retired (6 per cent of whom had retired after age 65) and in the plans of those currently at work (15 per cent of whom intended to retire late).

Preferences and attitudes

The preferences as opposed to the plans or actual behaviour of the entire sample aged 55-69 showed that substantial minorities wished to change their current employment status: 37 per cent of those at work wished to retire as soon as possible while 26 per cent of the non-employed (the retired, those in home duties and others) wished to take up some paid work. The latter group is larger in absolute terms than the former, so that if all older individuals were able to act on these preferences, there would be a small net increase in the numbers of people at work. However, the precise significance of this increased participation cannot be predicted from the current results, since it would entail complex trade-offs between full-time and part-time employment and might have little overall impact on the number of person-days of labour supplied.

The attitudes of the retired and those in home duties to their current situation were for the most part extremely favourable. Within these two groups, those who wanted a change were found to be significantly less satisfied with their current situation, but it was not the case that they were *dissatisfied*. Even the retired who wanted paid work gave no indication that they wanted anything like a reversal to their pre-retirement position.

Satisfaction with retirement was found to be strongly linked to financial position, health status and circumstances of retirement (ie satisfaction was higher where retirement was a positive life choice). Previous occupation was also associated with satisfaction with retirement – those from professional/managerial and other non-manual jobs were most likely to have a favourable view of retirement. Therefore it is not the case that those with more rewarding jobs miss employment the most. It would appear that differences in resources may provide a better account of these occupational differences.

Individual characteristics such as income, health status, marital status and education were not useful predictors of satisfaction among those in home duties. Only a desire for paid work was found to be linked to the satisfaction levels of this group.

Those in the 55 - 69 age group who were still in work generally viewed retirement in a positive light, looking forward to more freedom to do things they really wanted to do. However the majority (57 per cent) anticipated that they would miss the social aspect of employment. While over a third of the group wanted to retire as soon as possible and an even greater proportion (55 per cent) said they were only working for the money. This suggests that if financial incentives changed they would retire earlier.

Finally the group who were most dissatisfied with their current situation were those who were unemployed or permanently sick and disabled. Over a third of this group disagreed or strongly disagreed that being at home was very satisfying. A high proportion of the unemployed wanted to improve their situation by taking up paid work. However, this seemed a less likely escape option for the sick and disabled.

Gradual and flexible retirement

Looking at the relationship between what older workers would prefer and what the present retirement system offers, the most significant patterns arise in relation to gradual retirement. Approximately seven out of ten of those currently at work in the age range 55-69 would prefer to retire more gradually than is normal in the present system. This desire is consistent across those planning to retire early and those planning to retire at normal age and across the main occupational categories.

Among those who are already retired, a somewhat smaller proportion – less than half – say that in retrospect they would have preferred to have retired more gradually than they actually did. There is also a significant minority of retired people (between one fifth and a quarter) for whom lack of flexibility in either the pension system or employer practices hampered them from retiring at the age or pace they would have preferred.

These findings would suggest that any effort to adjust the present pension and retirement system to suit the preferences of older workers should pay a great deal of attention to mechanisms which allow for gradual and flexible retirement. It is not possible from the information gathered for the present study to assess what impact such mechanisms might have on the overall labour supply. Under a gradual or flexible retirement system, workers would be likely to reduce their labour time earlier than they would under the present more rigid system, but they might compensate by continuing to work beyond the present normal retirement age. It is quite possible, therefore, that given the right mix of incentives the overall net effect on the labour supply would be neutral but that otherwise an important gain would be achieved because retirement patterns would more closely match the preferences of workers.

Women in the home

Those who are neither at work nor retired consist principally of women in home duties who for the most part have been detached from the labour force for a long time (over a third have never had a paid job and a further 37 per cent have been out of paid work since before their mid-thirties). Three quarters of these have no desire to take up paid work, citing the attractions or demands of working in the home as the main reasons. A quarter of women in home duties say that would like to take up paid work, and this desire is strongest among those who have been in paid work at some time after age 50. The main obstacles they point to as reasons for not having a paid job is their lack of work experience and skills and employers' preference for younger workers.

Voluntary activity

One in three 55-69 year olds participates in the activities of voluntary organisations (that is, excluding informal helping activity between neighbours or relatives). These voluntary activists contributed an average of over six hours voluntary work per week. Voluntary activity of this kind was more common among those with paid employment (particularly among those who were partially employed and partially retired) than among those who had no paid work.

Education and training

Less than one in five (18 per cent) of the retired had taken a pre-retirement course. Though this proportion is low, it represents an increase since the early 1980s. Apart from pre-retirement courses, participation in other forms of training or education was low and was largely confined to participation in job-related training among those still at work.

Key policy implications

The most striking policy-relevant finding from the present study is the widespread preference among workers for gradual retirement. The present system causes retirement to act as a sudden guillotine on working life. The vast majority of workers would prefer a different system which would allow them to wind down their working life gradually before stopping completely. Therefore, there is a strong case for devising a pension and retirement system which would allow workers to fulfil that preference on a wide scale, particularly since it would appear feasible to do so in a way which would have a neutral impact on pension costs and the overall labour supply. It might be possible, for example, to facilitate partial retirement and entitlement to partial pensions before normal retirement age which could be compensated for by partial extension of working life beyond normal retirement age. Many practical difficulties in such a scheme could be envisaged but these may be amenable to imaginative solutions. In any event, such provisions deserve to be explored a great deal further and the widespread desire for gradual retirement needs to be noted as a major concern for future policy on pensions and retirement age.

A second major implication arises from the widespread incidence of sickness and disability as causes of early retirement. Some of the reported incidence in this area may be a disguise for other reasons for early retirement, such as inability to find work or disaffection with the kind of work which is available. However, evidence on reported illness among those citing this reason for early retirement suggests that underlying health problems are widespread and are a serious impediment to an active working life. While the primary implications of this pattern arise in the field of health policy, there may also be scope to take remedial measures in the field of employment policy, particularly in regard to the provision of semi-sheltered or flexible employment for those with health problems. Again, the point to be made here is not that improvements in the working or retirement situations of workers affected by sickness or disability are obvious or easily made but that the issue needs greater attention in policy relating to the employment circumstances of older workers.

As a final point, the present survey indicates that the older population does not contain a large reservoir of untapped labour supply. There are many older people at present not in paid work who would like to take up paid jobs, but their significance for the labour supply is counter balanced by the large numbers of older workers who would like to retire as soon as possible. If pensions and retirement systems for older people were made more flexible so as to facilitate movement over and back across the boundary between employment and retirement, the net effect on the labour supply of these counter balancing tendencies would probably be slight. This is not to say that such flexibility is thereby unnecessary or unimportant, since apart from any effects it might have on the labour supply, it could help fulfil the preferences of many older people and so lead to valuable gains in their quality of life.

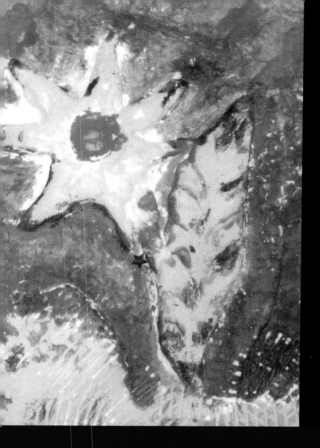

Chapter 1

Introduction

Chapter 1
Introduction

1.1 Background and purpose of study

Over recent decades in all developed countries health and life expectancy among older people have steadily improved. At the same time, retirement age has generally either remained stable or declined. The consequence is an increase in the proportion of the lifetime spent in retirement and rapid growth in the numbers of fit and active older people who have permanently departed the labour force.

Many people, both elderly and non-elderly, would regard this as a good thing, based on a view of retirement as a well-deserved reward which older people have earned through long years of work and contribution to society. However, there is a concern that, while retirement may be positive in most respects, it may not always reflect the interests or preferences of older workers. Some may retire not because they want to but because pressures or constraints of various kinds (such as lack of appropriate jobs, unsuitable working conditions, lack of necessary education or skills, or ageist attitudes among employers) may leave them with little alternative and may result in a worsening of either their standard of living or their satisfaction with life. Furthermore, widespread early retirement may not always be good for society: it may exacerbate labour shortages and so weaken economic progress, or it may increase the size of the retired population relative to the working population in such a way as to place strains on the fiscal and financial basis of pension schemes.

It is in this context that the National Council on Ageing and Older People has commissioned the present study of employment and retirement among older workers and retired people. Much of the international research on the transition to retirement and the factors which have caused retirement age to decline utilise statistical analysis of the correlates of the retirement decision (for a recent review of this research and its relevance to Irish circumstances, see Fitzgerald 2001). The present study, in contrast, looks more directly at the experiences and subjective preferences of older people. In other words, it focuses on the perspective of the older workers and retired people themselves on issues of work and retirement.

The objectives of the study are:

- to examine the meaning of work and retirement for older people, with particular reference to their participation in society and the capacity of work to promote physical and mental well-being

- to explore the potential and interest among older people in terms of participation in economic and voluntary activity

- to describe older people's preferences regarding participation in the labour force and the factors associated with the continuation of working life beyond retirement age among some older workers

- to outline older people's perceptions of barriers to participation in the labour force and the sensitivity of the workplace to the needs of older workers

- to examine older people's view on how employment practices and policies (including flexible retirement and flexible workplace practices) might be revised so as to facilitate their participation in the labour force

- to assess the policy of fixed retirement age from the perspective of older people and to draw out other implications.

1.2 Focus on 55-69 year olds

An analysis of data from the 1997 Labour Force Survey (LFS) which was carried out in advance of the study showed that in Ireland the transition from work to retirement takes place mainly in the age range between the late 50s and the late 60s. Table 1.1, which is drawn from the 1997 LFS, sets out the principal economic status of the population in the age range 55-69. This table shows that among men in the first third of that age range (that is, in the age group 55-59), a small minority – 13.1 per cent – had retired. This rose to a large majority – 70.6 per cent – in the final third of the age range, that is, in the age group 65-69. Permanent sickness and disability were almost as important as retirement as a cause of withdrawal from the labour force among men in the younger age group (it affected 11.5 per cent of men aged 55-59) though it declined in significance as retirement proper took over in the older age groups.

Patterns among women were quite different. Home duties was by far the most important economic status among women across the entire age range 55-69. Less than a quarter of women aged 55-59 were in paid work, while less than one in five of women aged 65-69 classified themselves as retired. This suggests that for women at or around retirement age in Ireland at present, the very concepts of work and retirement have quite a different significance from what they have for men.

In view of these patterns, a research approach which focused on those aged 55-69 seemed the most relevant to the concerns of the study. Furthermore, given the large proportion of women in that age range who were in home duties and therefore were neither in paid work nor retired, it seemed desirable to extend the scope of the study beyond paid work and retirement in the usual sense to include the population working in the home.

Table 1.1 Principal economic status of persons aged 55-69, Ireland 1997

	Males				Females				All
	55-59	60-64	65-69	Total	55-59	60-64	65-69	Total	
	Per cent								
At work	64.5	48.5	23.0	45.7	23.4	15.3	4.5	14.3	29.9
Unemployed	9.6	6.4	0.9	5.7	1.3	0.5	0.2	0.7	3.1
Home duties	0.8	1.3	1.3	1.1	68.1	72.7	74.5	71.9	36.8
Retired	13.1	32.3	70.6	38.0	4.1	8.9	19.4	10.9	24.3
Sickness/ disability	11.5	11.1	4.0	9.0	2.7	2.3	1.0	2.0	5.5
Other	0.5	0.5	0.2	0.4	0.4	0.4	0.4	0.4	0.4
Total	100	100	100	100	100	100	100	100	100

Source: 1997 Labour Force Survey microdata

The survey on which this report is based was carried out by the ESRI Survey Unit in the period February-May 2001.

The survey sample consisted of 817 persons aged 55-69 who were identified and interviewed during the February, March, April and May rounds of the ESRI's Monthly Consumer Survey (MCS). The MCS is a telephone survey of a national probability sample of 1,500 households carried out every month on behalf of Eurostat, the statistical agency of the EU. Each round of the survey yielded an average of just over 200 persons in the target age range for the present study, giving a completed sample of 817 persons (Table 1.2). A questionnaire module dealing with work and retirement, which was designed for the present study, was added as a supplement to the MCS and was administered by telephone to each of these of 817 persons. This module was divided into four main sections, one dealing with socio-demographic items and the other three targetted on distinct sub-groups within the sample, namely, (1) those at work, (2) the retired, and (3) those in home duties or otherwise not in the labour force.

Table 1.2 Achieved sample for retirement survey over four months of ESRI's Monthly Consumer Survey 2001

	N	%
February	167	20.4
March	234	28.6
April	200	24.5
May	216	26.4
Total	817	100.0

The sample has been weighted by age, sex, household size and region, using data on the national population aged 55-69 supplied by the CSO from the Quarterly National Household Survey for Quarter 2 December 2000.

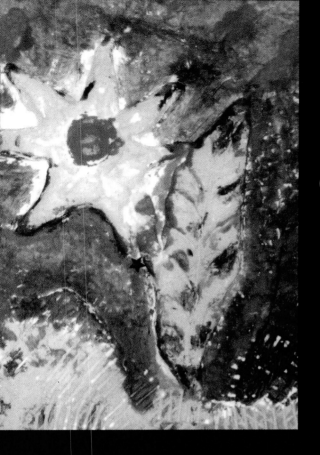

Chapter 2

Retirement Age

27

Chapter 2
Retirement Age

2.1 Introduction

This chapter focuses on age at retirement among workers aged 55-69 – actual retirement age among those who are currently retired and planned retirement age among those still at work. Its purpose is to establish patterns of early, late and normal-age retirement, the types of workers most likely to follow each retirement path and the reasons given for each path.

2.2 Employment status

The likelihood that respondents will be either retired or at work differs strongly by gender (Table 2.1). Nearly all of the men in the sample are either retired (49.4 per cent) or at work (43.2 per cent). Among women, by contrast, over half (53 per cent) are in home duties and only 18 per cent are retired, with 24 per cent at work. It is notable also that among men at work, the share who are self-employed is unusually large (23 per cent, compared to 26 per cent who are employed). This is in keeping with the well recognised tendency for the self-employed to work on to later ages than employees.

Table 2.1 Employment status of persons aged 55-69

	Males	Females	All
		%	
At work:	49.4	24.1	36.7
Self -employed	23.1	6.0	14.5
Employee	26.3	18.1	22.2
Unemployed	2.8	1.0	1.9
Home duties	1.3	53.0	27.3
Retired	43.2	18.1	30.6
Other	3.4	3.8	3.6
Total	100	100	100
N	378	439	817

2.3 Retirement age

Our sample of 817 individuals over the age of 55 contains 252 who have retired and 287 who are still at work. Table 2.2 presents actual (in the case of the retired) and planned (in the case of those at work) ages at retirement for these two sub-samples. The two groups cut across the age range in the sample (55-69) and so do not properly represent the age patterns of retirement by age cohort. To approximate more closely to age cohort patterns, we also present data on retirement age for two age sub-groups – those aged 65-69 in the case of the retired (ie those in the sample closest to having completed the transition to retirement) and those aged 55-59 in the case of those still at work (ie the age sub-group least likely to have made the transition to retirement). However, it should be kept in mind that neither of these age sub-groups as represented in Table 2.2 fully reflects its age cohort, since a small proportion of those aged 65-69 have not yet retired and so are omitted from calculations of actual retirement age, while a somewhat larger proportion of those aged 55-59 have already retired and so are omitted from calculations of planned retirement age.

Table 2.2 Age of actual and planned retirement

	Retired (actual)		At work (planned)	
	All ages	65-69 year-olds	All ages	55-59 year-olds
	%		%	
54 or under	14.0	8.1	–	–
55-59	26.0	11.1	3.4	6.6
60	12.3	12.0	12.4	22.7
61 to 64	18.4	23.4	7.8	6.0
65	17.9	30.2	28.5	27.2
Over 65	6.4	8.7	15.4	9.9
Don't know	5.1	6.6	32.5	27.7
N	252	148	287	159
Mean Age[1]	59.2	61.6	64.0	63.0

[1] Mean age is calculated excluding the 'don't knows.

With these caveats in mind, the data reveal a wide dispersion in retirement age among those currently retired (cf. Whelan and Whelan, 1988). Across the full age range of retired, only 18 per cent had left work at the supposedly standard age of 65. A high proportion had retired under age 60: 14 per cent had already retired by age 54 and a further 26 per cent retired between ages 55 and 59. Only 6.4 per cent had retired after age 65. The mean age for retirement was 59.2 years. Looking at the retired aged 65-69, the dispersion was somewhat narrower but still the proportion who had retired at the standard age of 65 was only 30 per cent. Over 30 per cent had retired by age 60 and the average retirement age was 61.6 years.

Given that such a high proportion have taken early retirement, it is interesting to note the difference between the actual retirement age and the compulsory age of retirement for each individual's occupation. Table 2.3 again shows the average age of retirement for those who have left the labour force and the expected retirement age for those still at work. It also compares those retirement ages with the average compulsory age of retirement for those whose occupations had compulsory retirement provisions (the latter numbered 41 per cent of all workers/retired in the sample). Those already retired have on average retired at just under age 60, approximately four years earlier than the compulsory retirement age for those with compulsory retirement provisions. The planned retirement age of those still at work is considerably higher, at approximately 64 years, and is only marginally below compulsory retirement age.

Table 2.3 Actual/planned retirement age v compulsory retirement age

	Retired (actual)		At work (planned)	
	Male	Female	Male	Female
Average actual/planned age	59.7	58.7	64.2	63.9
Average compulsory age*	63.9	64.2	65.2	65.3

* Note: relates to the 40 per cent of workers/retired who were in occupations with compulsory retirement provisions.

Respondents who were retired or at work were asked if they would consider their retirement age (whether actual or planned) to be normal, early or late for their occupation. The results again show the high incidence of early retirement among those who had already retired and the dominance of normal-age retirement in the plans of those who were still at work (Table 2.4).

Table 2.4 Early, normal and late retirement among the retired (actual) and those at work (planned)

	Retired (actual)			At work (planned)		
	Male	Female	All	Male	Female	All
Early	54.8	57.9	55.7	21.9	14.6	19.7
Normal	42.0	35.2	40.0	65.2	71.0	66.9
Late	3.1	7.0	4.3	12.9	14.4	14.4
Total	100	100	100	100	100	100
N	165	79	244	131	65	196

2.4 Characteristics of early retirement

Previous research has found that early retirement is more common among manual than white-collar workers (Whelan and Whelan 1988, p. 20). Table 2.5 explores this issue first by classifying actual (among the retired) and planned (among those at work) early retirement by level of completed education. (The sample numbers for those who report their retirement as late are too small to analyse separately.) Among the retired, those with third level education had the lowest incidence of early retirement (at 50.9 per cent), though the differences with other educational levels on this item were small. On the other hand, among those still at work, those with third level education were substantially more likely than other educational categories to plan to retire early (at 32.3 per cent). In other words, the best educated were most likely to plan to retire early but were somewhat less likely to actually do so than other educational categories. The reverse pattern held among those with primary education only: they were most likely to actually retire early (at 55.6 per cent) but least likely to plan to do so (at 11.9 per cent).

Despite these patterns, the link between level of education and actual retirement age is not strong. At all levels of education, higher proportions enter actual early retirement than the retirement plans of those still at work would lead one to expect.

The high incidence of early retirement among the retired in all educational categories is more striking than the relatively small differences on this item between the educational categories.

Table 2.5 Early retirement (actual and planned) by education level

	Primary	Inter/Cert Group	Leaving Cert	Third Level
	% retiring early			
Retired (actual)	55.6	67.4	52.4	50.9
N (unweighted)	87	48	54	60
At work: (planned)	11.9	20.8	15.5	32.3
N (unweighted)	83	62	77	63

Level of education is strongly linked to occupation and so we would expect similar patterns in occupational differences in retirement age. Table 2.6 presents the percentages in each occupational class entering retirement or expecting to retire at an early or normal age respectively. This shows that manual workers are more likely to enter early retirement (62.2 per cent), although only 14.3 per cent of current manual workers expect to retire early. As we would expect, the smallest proportion taking early retirement are self-employed or farmers.

Table 2.6 Early retirement (actual and planned) by occupational group

	Professional	Self-employed and farmers	Manual	Non manual
	% retiring early			
Retired (actual)	58.7	42.5	62.2	52.4
N (unweighted)	69	28	77	61
At work (planned)	31.0	20.5	14.3	8.4
N (unweighted)	51	51	55	37

It is possible that professional workers would stay in the labour force longer than manual workers because they enjoy better working conditions and because their jobs are likely to be less physically demanding. On the other hand, they may have wider access to occupational pensions which would make early retirement more financially feasible. According to the present data, 59 per cent of this group have retired early, and among those still in work, the professional/managerial group are somewhat more likely to have early retirement plans (though the small numbers of cases involved make generalisations unreliable). High rates of early retirement among manual workers may reflect greater vulnerability to 'involuntary' retirement. Table 2.7 shows that having an occupational pension is positively associated with plans for early retirement, but it is not related to actual early retirement. This again suggests that for many workers early retirement is unplanned.

Table 2.7 Occupational pension

	Receives occupational pension	No occupational pension
	% retiring early	
Retired (actual)	53.8	57.6
N (unweighted)	107	103
At work (planned)	24.8	13.7
N (unweighted)	59	94

2.5 Causes of early retirement

Among those who have already retired it is of interest to know if the point of retirement was chosen by the employee in other words 'did they jump or were they pushed?' Table 2.8 outlines the reasons given for early retirement. This shows that the most common reason given for early retirement is illness or disability, which applies to just under a third of the group. This can be seen as involuntary in the sense that the respondent is likely to have little control over it. The second most common reason reflects a voluntary decision based on financial incentives – workers were offered a good package to leave early and chose to do so. Those who said they retired early because they could afford to might also be added to this group, bringing it to 28 per cent of the total. One in ten respondents retired early because the work became too demanding or stressful, which again can be seen as a negative 'push' factor. Cases in which departure from employment was voluntarily chosen in order to take on other activities, including caring, were much less common and altogether amounted to 12 per cent of the total.

Among those who are still at work but planning to retire early, the reasons outlined are generally more positive. A quarter of respondents say they will retire early because they will get a good package or can afford to, while 32 per cent anticipate retiring early to pursue other activities. This greater positivity may arise because in general one cannot anticipate redundancy or a future illness. However, 23 per cent of the group plan to retire early because they believe that work will become too demanding or stressful for them.

Table 2.8 Main reasons for early retirement

	Retired	Still at work (planned retirement)
		%
Illness/disability	31.3	8.7
Involuntary redundancy	6.9	2.6
Package - retire early/vol redundancy	19.7	9.1
Could afford to	8.5	15.9
Work too demanding/stressful	10.0	23.4
To care for other family member	5.7	2.1
Spend more time with partner/family	1.3	3.2
To pursue other interests	4.5	26.6
Other reason	12.2	8.3
N (unweighted)	130	36

Figure 2.1 Reason for retiring early among currently retired

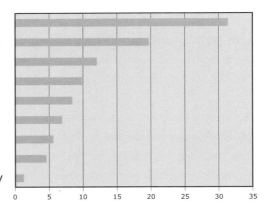

Illness/disability
Retire early/vol redundancy package
Other reason
Work too demanding/stressful
Could afford to
Involuntary Redundancy
To care for other family member
To pursue other interests
Spend more time with partner/family

0   5   10   15   20   25   30   35

2.6 Early retirement through sickness/disability

A prominent issue of debate in the EU over recent years is the extent to which exits from the labour market through sickness and disability schemes are in fact disguised unemployment. Here we explore this issue by examining the health status and voluntary activity levels of those who say they retired for reasons of sickness or disability. We also compare the responses of a much smaller category of respondents who define their current status as long-term sickness/disability. The number of cases in the relevant categories of the sample are small, but because of the interest of the topic the patterns they reveal are nevertheless worth looking at.

The health status of those who retired early due to illness is found to be significantly worse than for the general population in the 55-69 age group: 74 per cent of this group have a chronic physical or mental health problem compared to 24 per cent within the sample as a whole (Table 2.9). However the incidence of chronic ill health is not quite as high as among those who describe themselves as permanently sick or disabled (though again, small sample numbers raise doubts about the significance of these comparisons). Of those with health problems, two thirds report that this hampers their daily activities to some extent and 14 per cent report that their activities are severely hampered. The remaining 20 per cent have an illness that does not hamper their current daily activities. These levels of impairment are similar to those in the sample as a whole who report that they have health problems. The long-term sick/disabled report the highest levels of debilitating health problems.

Table 2.9 Any chronic physical/mental health problems?

	Retired early due to illness/disability	Long-term sick/disabled	Total sample
No	26.3	16.6	76.6
Yes:	73.5	83.4	23.4
Of which: Activity hampered?			
Severely	*13.9*	*28.9*	*17.7*
To some extent	*65.7*	*66.7*	*60.6*
No	*20.4*	*4.4*	*21.6*
Total	100.0	100.0	100.0
N unweighted	(42)	(27)	(807)

A similar pattern is observed when we look at the level of activity among different groups: those who have retired due to illness are less active than the population in general but are marginally more active than the long-term sick/disabled (Table 2.10). A third of all respondents are involved in voluntary work, but this drops to 21 per cent among those who have retired early due to illness and to 17 per cent among the long-term sick/disabled. Furthermore only 5 per cent say that they are retired but doing some paid work compared to 14 per cent of other early retired individuals (not shown).

Table 2.10 Involvement in voluntary activity

	Retired early due to illness	Long-term sick/disabled	Total sample
Yes	20.7	16.6	33.3
No	79.3	83.4	66.7
Total	100.0	100.0	100.0
N unweighted	(42)	(27)	(815)

These results suggest that the majority of those retiring early due to illness do have health problems that would limit their ability to do certain types work. However, they also point to the possibility that some of the groups would be able to take on less demanding activities. This suggests that sickness and disability may not represent absolute barriers to taking on paid work, even among those who give these factors as reasons for not being in a paid job at the present time. It is possible, rather, that the impact of sickness and disability on employment is at least partially contingent on the types of jobs available and the degree to which these are structured around fully fit workers. Thus there may be some scope for reducing the barrier effect of sickness and disability by restructuring jobs so that less demanding activities become separately available to workers who otherwise would have to stay out of work for what might amount to only moderate levels of sickness or disability.

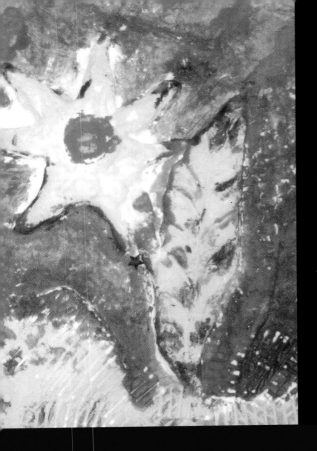

Chapter 3

Attitudes to Work and Retirement

Chapter 3
Attitudes to Work
and Retirement

In the preceding chapter we examined people's retirement age, a key aspect of people's retirement behaviour. In this chapter we explore older people's general attitudes and motivations regarding work and retirement. We look in particular at the degree to which they would prefer to change their current situation either by taking up paid employment (if they are not currently at work) or by retiring (if they are at work). We also explore general orientations to employment and retirement by examining respondents' satisfaction with different aspects of their current status.

3.1 Desire for change

The first step in drawing out people's general views regarding work and retirement is to establish the extent to which they want to change their current situation as far as paid work is concerned. How many people who are at work want to retire and how many people who are not at work (retired, in home duties, unemployed, sick or disabled) want to take up paid work? Table 3.1 provides information on this question, drawing on a range of items in the survey questionnaire.[1]

Overall, 30 per cent of respondents express a preference for changing their current employment status. Unsurprisingly, the unemployed are the group where the largest proportion wish to change, since unemployment is usually a sign of involuntary exclusion from employment (note, however, the very small number of unemployed in the present sample which makes generalisations about this group unreliable). The group least likely to want to change are those in full-time home duties – only

1   Respondents who are considered as desiring to change are identified as follows: those at work who 'agree' or 'strongly agree' that they would like to retire as soon as they can; those in in home duties, unemployed or sick/disabled who said they would like to take up a paid job, either full-time or part-time; and the retired who agree or strongly agree that 'even now I would like to take up some paid work'. For retirees doing some paid work (n=38) we used information on the desire to 'retire as soon as possible' or disagreement with the statement that they would like paid work to identify those desiring to change.

21 per cent of this group would like to be employed. Over a third of those currently at work would like to retire as soon as they can, but this is counterbalanced by the 29 per cent of the retired who would like to take up some paid work. The 'other' category consists mostly of people who define themselves as sick or disabled, and taking up a paid job appears not to be an option for most of this group.

Table 3.1 Percentage of respondents who would like to change their current employment situation

	Self-emp	Employee	Unemp	Home duties	Retired	Other	Total
No	64.1	62.6	53.3	78.1	71.0	79.3	70.0
Yes	35.9	37.4	46.7	21.9	29.0	20.7	30.0
Total	100.0	100.0	100.0	100.0	100.0	100.0	100.0
Unweighted N	103	181	13	231	246	29	803
Weighted N	64,413	98,499	8,495	120,330	134,950	15,815	442,502

In general, a higher proportion of those in employment wish to stop than of the non-employed who want to work. However, since the number of non-employed in the sample is substantially larger than the number at work, the number of non-employed who want paid work is greater than the number of employed who want to retire. In the present instance, 132 cases (16.5 per cent of the sample) want to move from non-employment to employment, while 105 cases (13 per cent of the sample) want to move from work to retirement. Grossed up to population totals, this would translate into approximately 73,000 non-employed who want paid work compared to 59,900 workers who want to retire, leaving a net gain of some 13,000 workers in the labour force.[2] It is difficult to assess what this small gain in numbers of workers would translate into as far as working time is concerned given the complex mix of part-time and full-time working which would result. The most plausible conclusion is that the net change in total labour time would at most be marginally positive – and might be negative if the 'added' workers tend generally to opt for short-hours part-time jobs (see further Chapter 4 below).

2   In fact the net gain may be smaller as housewives are somewhat under-represented in the sample and the retired are over-represented, so that the desire for employment among the non-employed may be overstated.

Table 3.2 shows that it is the youngest age group who are most likely to want to alter their employment status – 39 per cent of those aged 55-59 would like to make such a change, those over 65 appear more content with their current status, with only 20 per cent expressing a preference for change.

Table 3.2 Desire to change employment status by age

	55-59	60-64	65-69	Total
No	61.2	70.0	79.7	69.9
Yes	38.8	30.0	20.3	30.1
Total	100.0	100.0	100.0	100.0

In the following sections we explore attitudes and preferences among three groups of people. First we look at those currently retired and examine their attitudes to life after retirement. Next we examine the attitudes of those still in employment and further explore their expectations for retirement. Finally, we outline the attitudes of those in full-time home duties. This final section also includes the responses of those who are unemployed or sick/disabled. However, due to small sample numbers we cannot carry out any detailed analysis of this group.

3.2 Satisfaction with retirement

Although 30 per cent or so of the retired say that they would like to take up some paid work, their attitudes toward retirement are generally positive. Just over 70 per cent of the retired say that they enjoy life more since they retired, while 77 per cent agree that not working gives them the opportunity to do things they really want to do. However, there is evidence that the retired miss the social contact that comes with employment (Table 3.3). It is interesting to note there is no gender difference in the response to these three statements[3] even though the experience of employment is usually highly gendered and that material well being during retirement can differ markedly between men and women (Ginn and Arber, 1998; Layte, Fahey and Whelan, 1999)

---

3   It should be remembered that the majority of older women define themselves as housewives rather than retired and so did not answer this set of questions.

Older People's Preferences for Employment and Retirement in Ireland

Viewing retirement as an opportunity to pursue other interests is also found to be related to income levels (Table 3.9). Those who most strongly endorsed the view that not working enabled them to do the things they really wanted to do had the highest mean household income, while those who disagreed had a significantly lower weekly income. No relationship was found between missing the social contact of work and income levels, which suggests that having additional resources does not counteract the loss of social contact that comes with retirement.

Table 3.9 Not working enables doing things really want to do, by equivalised household income

	Mean income	N
Disagree/strongly disagree	£204.30	33
Neither agree nor disagree	£241.30	16
Agree	£292.50	125
Strongly Agree	£301.80	48
Total	£277.60	224
Anova	F=2.38 p=.07	

Health status is found to be another important predictor of attitudes to retirements among those already retired.[6] This is consistent with previous findings that chronic ill-health among the elderly has a strong bearing on their general psychological outlook (in terms of happiness, strain, self confidence, feeling of self-worth etc. – Layte *et al.* 1999). Retirees with chronic health problems were less likely to view their retirement in a favourable light perhaps because their illness prevented them from making the most of their additional free time. More than twice as many of those in poor health responded negatively to the two items outlined in Table 3.10 compared to those with no such problems. Health was found to be unrelated to the extent to which retired respondents missed the social aspect of employment, so these results are not included in Table 3.10.

---

6   Health was assessed by a self-report measure which asked respondents if they had any chronic physical or mental health problem, illness or disability.

Table 3.10 Attitudes to retirement by health status

	Enjoy life more		Do things really want to do	
	Health problems	None	Health problems	None
Disagree	30.6	13.8	24.1	9.6
Neither agree nor disagree	11.8	9.0	6.9	9.0
Agree	41.2	48.5	54.0	55.1
Strongly agree	16.5	28.7	14.9	26.3
Total	100.0	100.0	100.0	100.0
Chi-square	p=.005		p=.008	

As mentioned above we expect that one's assessment of retirement will be influenced by the quality of previous work experience. One common hypothesis is that less rewarding jobs make retirement more attractive, so that satisfaction with retirement would be expected to be higher among those who were in manual employment.However, previous research in Ireland has contradicted this hypothesis and shown that people who have rewarding, enjoyable jobs also tend to have an enjoyable retirement (Whelan and Whelan 1988, pp. 36-39). We examine this issue in two ways. Firstly, we compare attitudes to retirement by previous occupational position. Secondly, we examine whether views of retirement differ for those who had a purely instrumental view of work compared to those who found some more intrinsic value in employment.

The findings confirm that those who had higher-level occupations are more satisfied with retirement (Figure 3.2). Retirees from professional/managerial occupations and other non-manual jobs are found to have the most favourable attitudes about retirement, whereas the manual classes and the self-employed have the least favourable attitudes.

Figure 3.2 Satisfaction with retirement by previous occupation

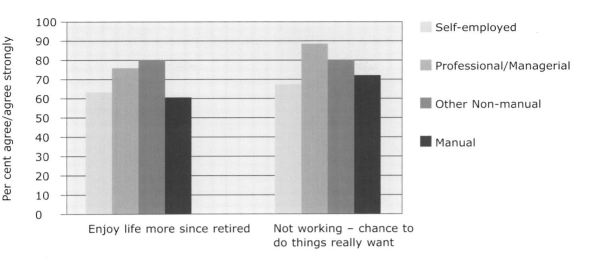

Finally we make a more direct test of whether employment commitment is related to retirement satisfaction. A common way of assessing employment commitment is to examine whether work is valued in itself rather than simply as a source of income (Warr, 1982; Russell, 1998). We expect that if respondents place an intrinsic value on employment, they may be less satisfied with retirement. To get at this concept of non-financial work commitment we asked respondents if they agreed/disagreed with the statement 'When I was working, I worked because I needed the money, not for any other reason'. Agreement with this statement indicates an instrumental view of employment whereas disagreement indicates employment commitment. Overall, commitment to employment was low among the retired (see Table 3.11) as previous research has predicted (Loscocco and Kalleberg, 1988; Russell, 1997). However, no relationship was found between having a purely instrumental view of employment and satisfaction with retirement among retirees (Table 3.12).

Table 3.11 When I worked I only worked for the money not for any other reason

	Per cent	n
Strongly disagree	3.4	9
Disagree	22.3	58
Neither agree nor disagree	9.7	25
Agree	50.6	131
Strongly agree	14.0	36
Total	100.0	259

Table 3.12 Retirement satisfaction score by non-financial employment commitment

Only worked for the money	Mean score	N
Disagree	9.8	66
Neither	9.4	25
Agree	9.3	167
Total	9.4	258

Scale=3-15, higher scores indicate greater satisfaction.

These results suggest that satisfaction with retirement among retirees is more dependent on current factors such as income and health than on people's previous work experience or commitment to employment. It is possible that the occupational results also reflect the influence of current resources rather than previous working conditions. Those from the professional/managerial occupations who are most satisfied with retirement are also those who are likely to have the greatest financial resources.

However, one non-current factor does appear to be influential and that is the circumstances in which the retirement decision was made. Where retirement was a positive life choice, retirement continues to be viewed in a more favourable light.

In the majority of cases, attitudes to retirement are highly positive among retirees. However, this does not mean that there are no aspects that respondents would not change. This is evidenced by the fact that 30 per cent of retirees would still like to have some paid work. We now turn to the views of those still in work and ask whether these attitudes are echoed by the currently employed or whether it is a case of the grass being greener on the other side?

3.3 Older workers: views of work and retirement

Those in employment were asked a range of questions designed to capture their views on work and their anticipated retirement. In Chapter 2 we outlined the expected timing of retirement for this group and here we look at issues which are more connected with the quality of work and retirement. Respondents were again asked whether they agreed or disagreed with a range of statements about work and retirement.

As mentioned at the start of this chapter, a significant percentage of 55-69 year olds currently at work would prefer to retire: 35 per cent agree that they would like to retire as soon as possible (Table 3.13) but the majority do not want to retire.

Those at work anticipate both positive and negative aspects of retirement (Table 3.13). The majority (68 per cent) believe that retirement will provide them with an opportunity to do things they really want to do, but an almost identical proportion expect that they will miss contact with co-workers when they retire. If we compare these responses to those of the retired in Table 3.3, we see that those at work have a somewhat more pessimistic outlook on retirement compared to those who have actually experienced retirement (77 per cent versus 55 per cent).

Table 3.13 Attitudes to work and retirement among the employed

	Like to retire as soon as I can	Will miss other people when retire	Time to do things really want to when retire	Work for money, no other reason
Strongly disagree	12.5	2.3	1.6	6.1
Disagree	40.8	23.9	16.3	29.3
Neither agree nor disagree	10.2	17.0	13.4	9.5
Agree	24.3	42.3	50.3	41.1
Strongly agree	12.3	14.6	18.3	14.0
Total	100.0	100.0	100.0	100.0
Base N	309	307	307	308

Older workers were also asked about their orientation to work to see if they had a purely instrumental view of work as a means of earning money, or if there was a non-financial commitment. More than half (55 per cent) of the employed agreed that they only worked for the money. This is lower than among the retired (65 per cent) which suggests that current workers are more committed to employment. If money is the only reason keeping a significant portion of older workers in their jobs it might be envisaged that better pension provision would lead to earlier retirements. (Because the number of cases is so small in the 'strongly disagree' category, subsequent analysis aggregates together the 'disagree' and 'strongly disagree' categories for these two measures.)

We tested whether these views varied according to the age-group of the respondent in the expectation that one's desire to retire might increase with age and that commitment to employment would decrease, as has been found in other studies of both the employed (Loscocco and Kalleberg, 1988) and the unemployed (Russell, 1997). However, only the item on missing social contact during retirement was found to vary with age. Those who are still working beyond what is considered normal retirement age, i.e. those in the 65-69 age group, are found to have the most negative views on social contact during retirement (see Table 3.14). This may be one factor why people in this group continue working even though they would be entitled to a state pension if they retired.

Table 3.14 Will miss being at work with other people when I retire

	55-50	60-64	65-69
Disagree/strongly disagree	29.0	24.5	16.7
Neither agree nor disagree	13.0	25.5	11.1
Agree	45.1	37.3	44.4
Strongly agree	13.0	12.7	27.8
Total	100.0	100.0	100.0
Chi-square		p=.02	

As the Irish workforce continues to be segregated by sex (Fahey, *et al.*, 2000) and men and women often experience different conditions at work (Barrett *et al.*, 2000; O'Connor, 1998) we might expect differences in the views of male and female workers on retirement.

Older female workers are found to have a greater level of non-financial employment commitment than older male workers. This indicates that many older female workers value certain aspects of work that could not be replaced by an adequate pension alone. One such factor may be the social interaction that comes with employment: female workers are found to be more concerned about losing social contacts with retirement than male workers (Figure 3.3).

Figure 3.3 Attitudes to work and retirement among currently employed by sex

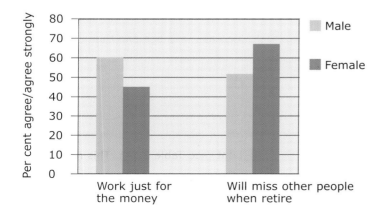

The proportion of older workers that are wedded to their jobs by reasons of finance alone tends to vary by occupational position. A purely instrumental attitude to work is most common among manual workers: almost 60 per cent of this group agreed that they only worked because they needed the money. This is consistent with previous research, which suggest that those with poorer working conditions will look for fulfilment outside employment (Walby,1986). More unexpectedly, many of the self-employed also held this view. These results suggest that the retirement decisions of these two groups of workers may be more sensitive to changes in financial incentives. It is interesting to note that household income is not directly linked to any of these attitudinal measures among the employed.

Figure 3.4 Instrumental attitude to employment by occupation

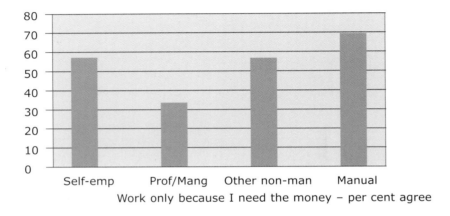

Work only because I need the money – per cent agree

3.4 Satisfaction among those in home duties and others

This final section considers the extent to which those in home duties and the unemployed and the sick/disabled people are satisfied with their current situation. The vast majority of those who define themselves as in home duties are women.[7] The situation of this group highlights the way in which the concept of retirement is gendered. Some of this group have previous work experience, but others have been outside the labour market for all or nearly all of their adult lives. Therefore for many there is no shift in identity or in daily activity when they reach the age of 65. Furthermore, the concept of retirement as a shedding of work obligations sits somewhat uneasily on those whose unpaid work continues unabated or in some cases increases as spouses or other relatives become infirm and require care.[8]

7   Only 5 of the 235 respondents in this group were male.

8   Both men and women around retirement age may find themselves in a position where caring work increases. However due to the traditional gap in the ages of husbands and wives and the lower life expectancy of men, women are likely to experience care provision more frequently.

Therefore among this group we did not ask about attitudes to retirement per se but rather about their views on having or not having a paid job.

These questions were also asked of those who defined themselves as unemployed, sick/disabled or other. Although this group may share common experiences with those who entered retirement due to sickness or involuntary redundancy, they did not identify themselves as retired in the present survey. Due to the small number in these categories they have been grouped together and no detailed analysis can be offered.

We saw above that those in home duties were the least likely to express a wish for any change in their employment position. This preference is reflected in the very positive evaluations of 'non-employment' expressed by this group (Table 3.13). More than 80 per cent of older women in home duties agree that being at home is very satisfying, while an overwhelming 97 per cent feel useful even though they don't have a paid job. Nor was there any sense that others looked down on them for not having a paid job, which is unsurprising given that full-time home duties is the norm for women of this age and generation in Ireland. The majority did not feel that they missed out on social interaction because they were not employed: just under 60 per cent disagreed that they missed being with other people at work compared to 38 per cent among the retired and just 26 per cent among those at work. However, when we look at housewives' views on whether not having a paid job allows them to do what they really want to do, their responses, although generally positive, are somewhat less favourable than those of the retired: 72 per cent of those in home duties agree/strongly agree compared to 77 per cent of the retired and 69 per cent of those at work.

Table 3.15 Views on not having a paid job among those in home duties 55-69 years

	Find being at home very satisfying	People look down on me - no paid job	Miss being with other people at work	Do things I really want without job	Feel useful with no job
Strongly disagree	0.0	16.3	8.4	1.0	0.0
Disagree	8.5	70.0	55.7	13.4	2.0
Neither agree nor disagree	7.0	8.4	12.8	13.4	1.0
Agree	61.2	3.9	21.2	56.9	57.7
Strongly agree	23.4	1.5	2.0	15.3	39.3
	100.0	100.0	100.0	100.0	100.0
N	201	201	201	201	201

The views of the unemployed and sick/disabled are found to be very much more negative than those of people in home duties (Table 3.16). Only a minority (42 per cent) saw being at home as satisfying or as an opportunity to pursue other interests (44 per cent), but the majority did not feel stigmatised (78 per cent) and felt useful without a job (91 per cent). This group expressed similar views about the loss of social contact as those still in employment, with 61 per cent saying they missed being with other people at work.

Table 3.16 Views on not having a paid job among the unemployed and sick/disabled 55-69 years

	Find being at home very satisfying	People look down on me - no paid job	Miss being with other people at work	Do things I really want without job	Feel useful with no job
Strongly disagree	18.2	9.4	9.1	3.1	0.0
Disagree	18.2	68.8	24.2	34.4	3.0
Neither	21.2	0.0	6.1	18.8	6.1
Agree	33.3	15.6	48.5	37.5	66.7
Strongly agree	9.1	6.3	12.1	6.3	24.2
	100.0	100.0	100.0	100.0	100.0
N	33				

We combine the responses to these five questions to create a measure of satisfaction with non-employment so that a higher score indicates greater satisfaction (Table 3.17). The scale ranges from 5-25 and has an alpha of .65. We examined the distribution of this score among those in home duties by a wide range of characteristics including age, household income, education level, health status, marital status and previous work experience (a job that lasted for at least one year). However, only the relationship with willingness to takeup employment proved significant. Those who wanted a paid job were found to have lower satisfaction scores than the rest of the group. This suggests that dissatisfaction with the home environment is a factor pushing these women into the labour market, which is a phenomenon found among younger women too (Russell, 2000). Note that the majority of those interested in work would like a part-time job.

Table 3.17 Satisfaction with non-employment by desire for paid work – if suitable work available

	Mean score	N
Would like a full-time job	16.4	6
Would like a part-time job	17.9	39
Would not like a job	20.0	152
Total	19.5	198

The desire to take up a paid job proved to be more strongly connected to respondents, characteristics than satisfaction with non-employment. Wanting a paid job was found to be related to previous employment experience (Table 3.18). Women in the 55-59 age group were significantly more likely to express an interest in taking up work than the older age groups.

Table 3.18 Home duties – want a job by previous employment experience

Want a paid job?	Had paid job outside home, lasting >1 yr?	
	No	Yes
No	87.2	72.2
Yes	12.8	27.8
	100	100

Wanting a paid job was also found to be related to age (Table 3.19).

The small number of respondents in the unemployed and sick/disabled categories prevent any further analysis of their responses. However it is worth noting that this group has the lowest mean equivalised household income: £220 per week compared to £314 for those at work, £282 for the retired and £234 for those in home duties. This economic disadvantage may well contribute to the low satisfaction levels observed among this group.

Table 3.19 Home duties – want a job by age

Want a paid job?	55-59	60-64	65-69
No	62.1	79.5	90.7
Yes	37.9	20.5	9.3
	100	100	100

3.5 Conclusion

This analysis has explored older people's general attitudes and motivations regarding work and retirement. We looked first at whether people would prefer to change their current situation either by taking up paid employment or by retiring.

A preference for changing one's current status was quite widespread, with 37 per cent of those at work expressing a wish to retire and 26 per cent of the non-employed wishing to take up some paid work. Given that the non-employed make up a greater proportion of the 55-69 age group than those at work (with an approximate ratio of 2:1), these results suggest that if all older individuals were able to act on their preferences regarding employment and retirement there would be a small net increase in employment. The precise level of this increased participation cannot be predicted from the current results, but the responses of those in home duties suggest that many of this group would only take up part-time work.

The findings on preferences for change should be interpreted in the light of the additional attitudinal responses outlined here. The attitudes of the retired and those in home duties to their current situation were for the most part extremely favourable. Within these two groups, those who wanted a change were found to be significantly less satisfied with their current situation, but it was not the case that these sub-groups were dissatisfied. Even the retired who wanted paid work did not appear to want a reversal to their pre-retirement position.

Satisfaction with retirement was found to be strongly linked to financial position, health status and circumstances of retirement (ie if retirement was a positive life choice). Previous occupation was also associated with satisfaction with retirement, in that those from professional/managerial and other non-manual jobs are most likely to have a favourable view of retirement. Therefore it is not the case that those with more rewarding jobs miss employment the most. It would appear that differences in resources may provide a better account of these occupational differences.

Individual characteristics such as income, health status, marital status and education were not useful predictors of satisfaction among those in home duties. Only a desire for paid work was found to distinguish the responses of this group. However, wanting a paid job was found to vary by age and by previous work experience. Younger women and those who had worked outside the home were more likely to want to take up paid work.

Those in the 55 to 69 age group who were still in work generally viewed retirement in a positive light, looking forward to more freedom to do things they really wanted to do. However, the majority (57 per cent) anticipated that they would miss the social aspect of employment. While over a third of the group wanted to retire as soon as possible an even greater proportion (55 per cent) said they were only working for the money. This suggests that if financial incentives changed they would retire earlier.

Finally the group who are most dissatisfied with their current situation are those who are unemployed or permanently sick and disabled. A high proportion of the unemployed want to improve their situation by taking up paid work. However, this seems a less likely escape option for the sick and disabled.

Chapter 4

Retirement and Work Preferences

Chapter 4
Retirement and Work Preferences

4.1 Introduction

Earlier chapters have looked at retirement age and at people's general attitudes and preferences regarding work, retirement and related issues. Here we continue with an analysis of preferences regarding work and retirement, focusing on people's perceptions of the present retirement system and possible obstacles in the labour market and pension/taxation system which might hamper them from pursuing their preferences.

4.2 Gradual retirement

As far as the current system of retirement is concerned, the aspect of retirement preferences which stands out most strongly among current and retired workers aged 55-69 is a widespread desire for gradual retirement in the form of reducing the number of hours or days worked per week before stopping completely. This preference is particularly strong among those who are still at work. As Table 4.1a shows, some 70 per cent of those at work either 'agree' or 'agree strongly' that they would like to retire gradually. Of those who are already retired, 44 per cent say that in retrospect they would have liked to have retired more gradually than they actually did.

Table 4.1a Preferences regarding gradual retirement among those still at work and the retired

'Prefer to retire more gradually'	At work	Retired	All
	%		
Strongly disagree	4.1	3.7	3.9
Disgree	18.4	39.0	27.8
Neither agree nor disagree	7.8	13.0	10.2
Agree	46.4	32.9	40.3
Strongly agree	23.2	11.4	17.8
Total	100	100	100
(N of cases)	(293)	(246)	(539)

Chi - square: p<0.001

It proved impossible in the context of a brief survey questionnaire to establish in detail what respondents meant by 'gradual' retirement – at what ages they would like the retirement process to begin and end, or how they would reduce working time (whether shorter working days, shorter working week or intermittent periods off work). However, an indication that 'gradual retirement' is not simply another way of speaking of early retirement can be gleaned from a cross-classification between the preference to retire gradually and the preference to retire as soon as possible (the analysis in this instance is limited to those still at work). This cross-classification suggests that the desire for gradual retirement is somewhat stronger among those who do not want to retire as soon as possible than among those who do, but it is quite high in both groups (Table 4.1b). In other words, substantial majorities prefer gradual retirement, whether they want to retire early or at normal age.

Table 4.1b Preference regarding gradual retirement classified by desire to retire as soon as possible among those still at work

'Prefer to retire more gradually'	'Like to retire as soon as possible'		
	Disagree	Neither agree nor disagree	Agree
	%		
Disagree	14.1	18.7	34.5
Neither agree nor disagree	8.0	18.8	4.4
Agree	77.9	62.6	61.0
Total	100	100	100
(N of cases)	(163)	(32)	(113)
Row per cent	52.9	10.4	36.7

Chi - square: p<0.01

A similar cross-classification (not reported here) between the preference for gradual retirement and the intention to retire early showed no statistically significant patterns. This too suggests that the preference for gradual retirement is not particularly associated with plans to retire either early or at the normal age.

4.3 Retirement age and flexible pension arrangements

Those who had already retired were asked whether they would have chosen a different retirement age if pension arrangements had been more flexible (This issue differs from gradual retirement in that it refers to age of retirement rather than whether retirement is spread out over a period or not.) Table 4.2 classifies the responses between early retirers and those who retired at normal age (late retirers in the sample were too few to examine separately). The results show that between a fifth and a quarter either agreed or agreed strongly that they would have retired at a different age if pension arrangements had been more flexible. There was no statistically significant differences between early and normal-age retirers on this item.

Table 4.2 Preferences regarding retirement at different age among retired, classified by normal-age and early retirement

'I would have retired at different age if pension arrangements were more flexible'	Normal-age retirers	Early retirers	All
		%	
Strongly disagree	4.7	5.5	5.2
Disagree	49.1	54.1	52.0
Neither agree nor disagree	23.6	15.8	19.0
Agree	19.8	20.5	20.2
Strongly agree	2.8	4.1	3.6
Total	100	100	100
(N of cases)	(106)	(146)	(252)

Chi - square: non-significant.

The retired were also asked about the extent to which they would have continued working rather than retire if their employers had been more accommodating (Table 4.3). A quarter either agreed or strongly agreed that they would have done so and, as with the previous item, there was no significant difference between early and normal-age retirers on this item.

Table 4.3 Preferences regarding continued working, contingent on more accommodating employer, among retired, classified by normal-age and early retirement

'I would have continued working rather than retire if my employer had been more accommodating'	Normal-age retirers	Early retirers	All
		%	
Strongly disagree	7.8	4.3	5.8
Disagree	43.7	46.4	45.3
Neither agree nor disagree	26.2	24.3	25.1
Agree	17.5	21.4	19.8
Strongly agree	4.9	3.6	4.1
Total	100	100	100
(N of cases)	(106)	(146)	252

Chi-sq: non-significant

These items suggest that there is a significant minority of retired people for whom lack of flexibility in either the pension system or employer practices hampered them from retiring at the age or pace that they would have preferred.

4.4 Women in home duties, the unemployed and the sick/disabled

As indicated earlier, those in the age-group 55-69 who are neither at work nor retired consist principally of women in home duties, although there are also small numbers of unemployed and sick/disabled. Most of this combined group have either never had a paid job or have been out of paid work for at least twenty years, while only 16.6 per cent have been in the paid workforce at any time since age 51 (Table 4.4). Thus their history of labour market attachment is weak.

Table 4.4 Job history of women in home duties, the unemployed and the sick/disabled aged 55-69

Age left last paid job	Per cent
Never had a paid job	35.7
25 or under	16.6
26-35	20.0
36-50	11.1
51+	16.6
Total	100.0
(N)	(236)

Almost one in four of this combined group say that they would like to take up paid work, in most cases with a preference for a part-time rather than a full-time job (Figure 4.1). The desire to take up paid work is weakest among those who never had a paid job or have been out of paid work for a long time, while it is relatively strong among those who had a paid job at some time since age 51 (Table 4.5).

Figure 4.1 Preferences regarding taking up paid work among those in home duties, the sick and those with disabilities (base N=243)

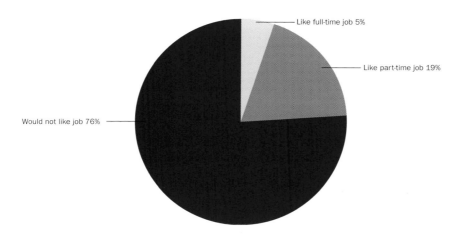

Like full-time job 5%

Like part-time job 19%

Would not like job 76%

Table 4.5 Per cent wishing to take up paid work by age left last paid job among those in home duties, the sick and those with disabilities

Age left last job	Per cent in each category	Per cent of each category wishing to take up paid work
Never had a paid job	36	13
25 or under	17	23
26-35	20	27
36-50	11	31
51+	17	41
Total	100	24
(N)	(236)	(55)

Chi - square: p<0.05

To assess the impact of the benefit/pension system on the orientation to paid work among this group, they were also asked if they agreed or disagreed with the statement 'I would do paid work if the benefit/pension system were more flexible'. The responses to this question among women in home duties are set out in Table 4.6, with a broad classification by educational level (the unemployed and sick/disabled are omitted because of their small numbers in the sample). These responses show that just over one in five women in home duties point to the pension/benefit system as a disincentive to taking up paid work, but there is no significant difference on this item between those with primary education only and those with secondary or higher education.

Table 4.6 Preferences regarding paid work, contingent on pension/benefit system, among those in home duties

'I would do paid work if the pension/ benefit system were more flexible'	Education level		
	Primary	Inter cert. or higher	All
		%	
Strongly disagree	14.3	3.6	8.5
Disagree	50.5	58.2	54.7
Neither agree nor disagree	14.3	12.7	13.4
Agree	19.8	22.7	21.4
Strongly agree	1.1	2.7	2.0
Total	100	100	100
(N)	(91)	(110)	(201)

Chi - square: non-significant

Figure 4.2 shows that the main reasons which women in home duties give for working in the home rather than in the paid labour force have to do with the attractions or demands of working at home – 79 per cent mention that they 'prefer to be at home' and 61 per cent claim being too busy at home. However, labour market difficulties also rate highly – 61 per cent report that they have been out of the workforce too long, 47 per cent cite lack of skills and 45 per cent mention employers' preference for younger workers. Other factors which might be expected to have an influence in fact turn out to be a consideration for very few. For example, the disincentive effect of income tax on taking up paid work or the possible impact on medical card or benefit entitlements is mentioned by only 16 per cent and the lack of transport is mentioned by only 14 per cent.

Figure 4.2 Reasons for not having a job among women in home duties who do not want to take up paid work (base N=172)

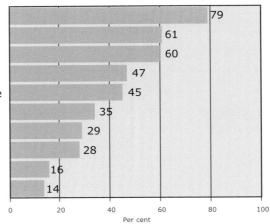

Reason	Per cent
Prefer to be at home	79
Too busy at home	61
Out of workforce too long	60
Don't have right skills	47
Employers want younger people	45
Lack the confidence	35
Health not good enough	29
No suitable jobs locally	28
Effect of tax, medical card	16
Have no transport	14

Among those who would like to take up paid work (Figure 4.3), the main reasons they give for not doing so concern a mismatch between their skills or job preferences and what they consider is in demand in the local labour market (though note that the number of sample cases on which these patterns is based is small). About half point to the lack of suitable jobs in the locality, their own lack of appropriate skills or employers' preference for younger workers as reasons. Lack of confidence and health problems are also mentioned by some, while the role of income tax or benefit effects, the lack of transport and a preference to be at home come at the bottom of the list.

Figure 4.3 Reasons for not having a job among those who would like to take up paid work (base N=57)

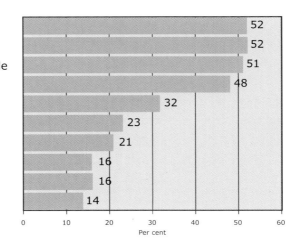

Reason	Per cent
No suitable jobs locally	52
Don't have right skills	52
Employers want younger people	51
No part-time jobs available	48
Lack the confidence	32
Health not good enough	23
Too busy at home	21
Have no transport	16
Effect of tax, medical card	16
Prefer to be at home	14

By far the strongest divergence between what older workers would prefer and what the present retirement system offers arises in relation to gradual retirement. Approximately seven out of ten of those currently at work in the age range 55-69 would prefer to retire more gradually than is normal in the present system. This desire is consistent across those planning to retire early and those planning to retire at normal age and across the main occupational categories.

Among those who are already retired, a somewhat smaller proportion – less than half – say that in retrospect they would have preferred to have retired more gradually than they actually did. There is also a significant minority of retired people (between one fifth and a quarter) for whom lack of flexibility in either the pension system or employer practices hampered them from retiring at the age or pace they would have preferred.

These findings would suggest that any effort to adjust the present pension and retirement system to suit the preferences of older workers should pay a great deal of attention to mechanisms which allow for gradual and flexible retirement. It is not possible from the information gathered for the present study to assess what impact such mechanisms might have on the overall labour supply. Under a gradual or flexible retirement system, workers would be likely to reduce their labour time earlier than they would under the present more rigid system, but they might compensate by continuing to work beyond the present normal retirement age. It is quite possible, therefore, that the overall net effect on the labour supply would be neutral but that otherwise an important gain would be achieved in that retirement patterns would more closely match the preferences of workers.

Those who are neither at work nor retired consist principally of women in home duties who for the most part have been detached from the labour force for a long time (over a third have never had a paid job and a further 37 per cent have been out of paid work since before their mid-thirties). Three quarters of these have no desire to take up paid work, citing the attractions or demands of working in the home as the main reasons. A quarter of women in home duties say that would like to take up paid work and this desire is strongest among those who have been in paid work at some time after age 50. The main obstacles they point to as reasons for not having a paid job is their lack of work experience and skills and employers' preference for younger workers.

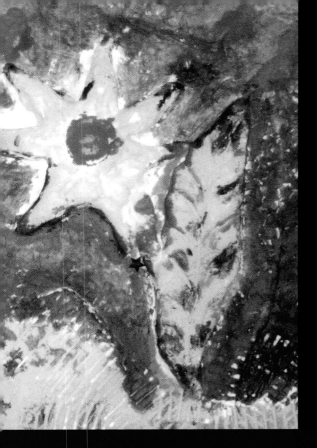

Chapter 5

Voluntary Activity and Training/ Education

73

Chapter 5
Voluntary Activity and Training/Education

In this chapter we explore respondents' involvement in voluntary activity and their participation in education, training and pre-retirement courses. Participation in voluntary activity is of interest because it has both individual and societal benefits. For those who are retired or otherwise not in the labour force, voluntary work might fulfil some of the psychological functions normally supplied by employment: the imposition of a time structure, regular shared experiences and contacts with people outside the nuclear family, involvement in collective goals, status and identity, and activity (Jahoda, 1982, p. 310).[1] There are also obvious societal benefits from the unpaid work that older people do. Furthermore there is a concern amongst community groups that increased labour market participation among certain groups, particularly women in the home, will deplete the number of volunteers and so mean that voluntary agencies will no longer be able to provide the services they currently supply. As we have seen from Chapter 2 above, such concerns are unlikely to apply to the over-55s since current trends and preferences suggest that their labour force participation is unlikely to increase in the future. Thus there is a particular interest in exploring the extent and nature of voluntary activity among 55-69 year olds.

The chapter also examines participation in education, job training and pre-retirement training. It does so from a number of perspectives: as an indication of interest in continuing employment; as an indicator of access to employment-related skills and training; as a measure of preparation for retirement, and as a source of fulfilment and activity for those aged over 55.

---

1   Warr (1987) identifies nine environmental features that influence mental health which may be found in work or in other activities: opportunity for control, opportunity for skill use, externally generated goals, variety, environmental clarity, availability of money, physical security, opportunity for interpersonal contact and valued social position.

In examining voluntary activity, we concentrate here on more formal or organised voluntary activity rather than the more informal pattern of help and exchange that exists between friends, relatives and neighbours (though see Chapter 4 above for an outline of the extent of care-giving among 55-69 year-olds to people inside or outside their own households). Respondents were asked whether they do any 'voluntary, unpaid work for any of the following organisations (eg sit on committees, organise events, do house visits, fund raise, do the books, etc.)?' and were then presented with a list of types of organisation – organisations for older people, young, people with disabilities or deprived; religious or church organisations; sports organisations; trade unions or professional association; political parties/groups; local community groups and others.

Exactly a third of those aged 55-69 years were involved in some sort of organised voluntary work (Table 5.1). On average those involved in voluntary work spend 6.3 hours on this activity per week. The majority of volunteers (61 per cent) devote four hours a week or less to this activity (Table 5.2). The median number of hours per week is three, and the mode was two hours per week (applying to 20.1 per cent of volunteers).

Table 5.1 Percentage involved in any voluntary work

	Per cent
Yes	33.4
No	66.6
Total	100.0
Base N	817

Table 5.2 Number of hours per week spent in voluntary work

Hours voluntary work per week	Per cent
1	16.6
2	20.1
3	13.3
4	11.1
5-10	28.1
11-25	8.0
Over 25	2.7
Total	100.0
Base N*	227

*   Applies to volunteers only and excludes fourteen missing cases

When we look at the type of activity engaged in by older voluntary workers, we see that they are most commonly involved in community groups or organisations dealing with the older people, youth, people with disabilities or deprived. The least commonly mentioned groups were political organisations and trade union/professional organisations. The data in Table 5.3 also suggest that some respondents are involved in more than one voluntary agency.

Table 5.3 Extent of voluntary work in different organisations

	Per cent doing vol. work	N
Orgs for youth, older people, disabled, deprived	11.1	91
Religious/church organisations	9.1	74
Sport organisations	6.2	50
Trade unions/professional organisations	1.8	14
Political parties/groups	1.6	13
Local community groups	11.1	90
Other	5.9	48

Note: Respondents could tick more than one organisational type.

There is no statistically significant difference in the proportion of men and women involved in voluntary work (35 per cent and 32 per cent respectively) nor in the amount of time men and women devoted to this work. Neither does involvement in voluntary activity decrease with age as we might expect: those in the youngest age group 55-59 are most active, but those in the eldest group (65-69) are the second most active (Table 5.4). Differences in the number of hours worked by age group were also statistically insignificant.

Table 5.4 Voluntary activity by age group

Involved in voluntary work?	55-59	60-64	65-69
Yes	36.9	29.1	33.5
No	63.1	70.9	66.5
Total	100.0	100.0	100.0
Base N	290	268	257

chi - square = not significant

Voluntary activity did vary with the employment status of respondents and their social class. The relationship between employment status and voluntary work does not support the argument that increased employment participation will reduce the capacity for voluntary activity in Irish society. In fact, among the 55-69 age group, the partially retired are the most likely to be involved in voluntary work, followed by the fully employed (Table 5.5). One possible explanation for this relationship is that those in employment are more likely to have resources and skills that are useful to the voluntary sector even if they do not have as much 'free' time. This explanation is often invoked to account for higher participation in the informal economy by the employed compared to the unemployed (Pahl, 1984, p.38). Those who are partially retired might have the ideal combination of time and resources to contribute to the voluntary sector.[3]

The 'other' group are least likely to participate in voluntary activity. As mentioned earlier this group is largely comprised of those who are sick/disabled and to a lesser extent the unemployed. Therefore ill-health is likely to prevent participation amongst this group (see Chapter 3). Better physical and mental health may also be one of the resources possessed by those still in employment and help account for their higher participation.

Table 5.5 Percentage involved in voluntary work by employment status

	Employed	Retired and some paid work	Fully retired	Home duties	Other
Yes	35.7	57.1	32.6	30.2	17.8
No	64.3	42.9	67.4	69.8	82.2
Total	100.0	100.0	100.0	100.0	100.0
Base N	297	35	215	222	45

Chi-square P=.004

Differences in resources may also account for the social class patterns observed in voluntary activity. The highest rates of participation in voluntary activity are observed among the professional/managerial and the other non-manual classes (Table 5.6). The participation rate among the self-employed is average, while

---

3   It is also possible that some of this group might have defined themselves as partially retired because of their voluntary work although the original question specified paid work.

participation among those who are or were in manual occupations is below average at 22 per cent. This relationship between social class and voluntary activity among the retired was also noted by Whelan and Whelan (1988). They found that 27 per cent of the higher white collar group engaged in such activity compared to only 8 per cent of non-skilled manual workers. The overall percentage involved in voluntary work is not reported by Whelan and Whelan but comparison with their data suggest that, if anything, there has been an increase in voluntary activity among this age group since the late 1980s. This cautions against any pessimistic view of a decline in the level of volunteering in Irish society.

Table 5.6 Percentage involved in voluntary work by occupational group*

	Self-emp.	Prof./managerial	Other non-manual	Manual
Yes	33.8	43.6	41.9	22.3
No	66.2	56.4	58.1	77.7
Total	100.0	100.0	100.0	100.0
base N	148	165	186	224

Chi-square P=.000

*   Occupation in current or last job, those with no employment experience are excluded

A similar pattern may be observed by educational level. Those with the highest educational qualifications are much more likely to be involved in voluntary activity than those with lower educational levels (Table 5.7). The proportion doing voluntary work varies from 55 per cent among those with third level education to 19 per cent among those with only primary level education.

Table 5.7 Percentage involved in voluntary work by educational level

	Primary	Inter Cert	Leaving Cert	Other 2nd level	3rd level
Yes	18.9	33.3	39.4	38.2	54.8
No	81.1	66.7	60.6	61.8	45.2
Total	100.0	100.0	100.0	100.0	100.0

Chi-square P<.001

The questionnaire also collected information on the extent of respondents' involvement in education and training, including specific questions on job-related training and pre-retirement courses (Table 5.8).

Table 5.8 Participation in training and education

	Yes	No	Base N
Participated in retirement preparation course*	18.4%	81.6%	223
Participated in job-related training in last 12 months	8.9%	91.1%	807
Participated in any other courses or education in last 12 months	9.4%	60.6%	795

* Figures relate to currently retired only

Just under one in five of the retired group (18 per cent) had participated in a pre-retirement course of some sort. This represents an improvement since the early 1980s when only 10 per cent of the retired had attended such courses (Whelan and Whelan, 1988, p. 133). However, it also means that the majority of the workforce still retire without the benefit of any formalised preparation. Whelan and Whelan's study noted that the courses available were often of very short duration and were usually attended very close to actual retirement, even though there was growing evidence that preparation should begin long before retirement in order to be truly effective (Whelan and Whelan, 1988, p. 49).

The current data also replicate Whelan and Whelan's finding that participation in a retirement preparation course was much more common in the professional/ managerial classes compared to manual workers (Table 5.9). However, our results show that participation is also high among other white collar workers and that the proportion of manual workers taking such courses has increased from 5 per cent in Whelan and Whelan's study to 15 per cent in the present study.

Table 5.9 Participation in pre-retirement courses by previous occupational position

	Self-emp	Prof/Mang	Other Non-man	Manual
Yes	3.3	25.4	25.0	15.1
No	96.7	74.6	75.0	84.9
Total	100.0	100.0	100.0	100.0

Apart from pre-retirement courses, participation in job related training and any other type of education is relatively uncommon among our respondents (Table 5.8). This is disappointing given the increasing emphasis on the benefits of life-long learning. As one would expect, involvement in job related training in the past twelve months was found to be strongly related to current employment status: 18 per cent of the employed, 11 per cent of the partially retired, 2 per cent of the retired and 4 per cent of those in home duties had undertaken such training. For those outside employment, low participation in job-related training must be seen as demonstrating a high commitment to employment. The low levels of participation among those outside employment may also reflect problems of access. Recent reports suggest that many of the courses available through state agencies are not accessible to older age groups.

Job training was also strongly linked to education level (21 per cent of those with third level qualifications had participated in such training compared to only 4 per cent of those with primary or Inter Certificate qualifications). Participation was also found to vary by occupational position. However, more complex modelling would be needed to establish whether these relationships arise because the better educated and those in higher non-manual positions remain in the workforce longer.

Only 9 per cent of the group had participated in any other type of education or training opportunities in the last twelve months. Participation rates were equal for men and women. However, participation declined with age: 14 per cent among 55-59s 9.2 per cent among 60-64s and 4.8 per cent among 65-69s.[4] The employed were significantly more likely to have undertaken education or training than any other group. Again this may reflect greater resources both in monetary terms (eg for course fees, materials, access to a car) and health terms which may facilitate access. Similarly those with higher education levels and those in white collar

---

4   Chi-square test, p=.002

occupations were much more likely to have participated in non-job-related education/training than those with lower qualifications and manual workers: 20 per cent of those with third level qualifications participated compared to 5 per cent of those with no qualifications, and 18 per cent of the professional/managerial group compared to 5 per cent of manual workers (in both cases the differences are statistically significant at the .001 level). These results suggest that access to educational opportunities remains highly unequal even in later life.

5.4 Conclusion

Older people continue to play a significant role in voluntary activity and, as far as it is possible to discern, the trend over time appears to have been towards greater participation rather than less. Furthermore it was those in employment and particularly those who were partially at work and partially retired who were most involved in voluntary activity. Therefore concerns that increased labour market participation among this age group might lead to a decline in volunteering appear to be unfounded on a number of grounds. If preferences for more gradual retirement were facilitated by policy, the numbers of partially employed would increase and, based on the present results, this would have a positive impact on voluntary activity. It appears that the partially retired have that apposite combination of time and resources which enables them to contribute heavily to voluntary activity. This is not to deny that work intensification in the form of long hours and the increased labour force participation among women under 55 may have an effect on volunteering, but these questions are beyond the scope of the current study.

The results on the level of participation in pre-retirement training, job-related training and other education are disappointing. Although there has been some increase in pre-retirement training the great majority of the retired still do not get any sort of formal preparation for this major life transition. Participation in job-related and other educational opportunities is even lower and continues to be highly divided. Further qualitative research could shed light on the reasons for this low rate of participation and highlight any access barriers that could be eliminated through policy action.

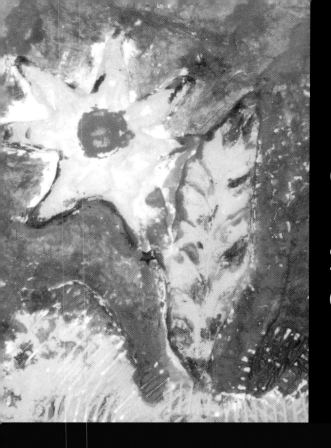

Chapter 6

Summary and Conclusions

Chapter 6
Summary and Conclusions

6.1 Main findings

The main findings from the survey data presented here may be listed as follows:

1. Early retirement is common. Among all retirees in the sample, over two thirds retired before age 65, with an average retirement age of approximately 59 years. The average age of retirement among 65-69 year-old retirees (the age-group in the sample closest to having completed the transition to retirement) was 61.6 years.

2. Early retirement is often unplanned in that the most common cause, which accounts for one third of early retirements, is illness or disability. The second most common cause, which accounts for a further 20 per cent of early retirements, is voluntary redundancy or early retirement packages (processes typically initiated from the employer's rather than the employee's side).

3. Those who cite sickness or disability as a reason for their early retirement report significantly worse health and higher levels of physical impairment than others in their age group.

4. About one third of those aged 55-59 plan to retire early, the majority of them at or before age 60.

5. Late retirement is much less common than early retirement and arises mainly among the self-employed.

6. Preferences are somewhat more pro-retirement than plans: 37 per cent of those still at work would *like* to retire as soon as possible, which is slightly higher than the proportion who *plan* to retire early.

7. The proportion of the retired and others not at work who would like to take up some paid work is lower (at 26 per cent) than the proportion of workers who would like to retire (37 per cent). On the other hand, the retired and others not at work outnumber those at work in the age range 55-69, so that the absolute number of those currently not in employment who would like to take up work is greater than the absolute number of workers who would like to retire. If preferences in these areas were to be fully acted on, there would be a small increase in the numbers at work. However, because of possible trade-offs between full-time and part-time work, the impact on the number of person-days of labour supplied is difficult to anticipate but would probably be slight.

8. Retirement is a positive state – the retired are generally quite satisfied with their current situational, although those who want paid work are somewhat less positive than those who do not want paid work.

9. There is a strong preference for gradual retirement among older workers that is gradually to reduce the number of hours or days worked before stopping completely. Approximately seven out of ten of those currently at work in the age range 55-69 would prefer to retire more gradually than is normal in the present system.

10. Flexible retirement (ie retirement at a different age than is allowed at present) is less of a concern than gradual retirement, but still is an issue for some.

11. About one in three people in this age group engage in voluntary activity and carry out an average of just over six hours voluntary work per week. Those who are in paid jobs (particularly those who are partially employed and partially retired) are more likely to carry out voluntary work than those who do not have paid jobs.

12. Less than one in five retired people have taken a pre-retirement course and take-up of other educational or training courses among 55-69 year olds is even lower.

Two major implications for policy follow from these findings:

- The first arises from the widespread preference among workers for gradual retirement. The present dominant system causes retirement to act as a sudden guillotine on working life. The vast majority of workers would prefer a different system which would allow them to wind down their working life gradually before stopping completely. It would be a complex task to devise a pension and retirement system which would allow workers to fulfil that preference on a wide scale without at the same time greatly increasing the overall cost of pensions. It might be feasible to facilitate partial retirement and entitlement to partial pensions before normal retirement age which could be compensated for by partial extension of working life beyond normal retirement age – that is, to allow for gradual retirement without reducing the number of person-years for which each worker is in employment. Many practical difficulties in such a scheme could be envisaged but these may be amenable to imaginative solutions. In any event, the point to be made here is that such provisions deserve to be explored a great deal further and the desire for gradual retirement needs to be noted as a major concern for future policy on pensions and retirement age.

- The second major implication arises from the widespread incidence of sickness and disability as a cause of early retirement. Some of the reported incidence in this area may be a disguise for other reasons for early retirement, such as inability to find work or disaffection with the kind of work which is available. However, evidence on reported illness among those citing this reason for early retirement suggests that underlying health problems are widespread and are a serious impediment to an active working life. While the primary implications of this pattern arise in the field of health policy, there may also be scope to take remedial measures in the field of employment policy, particularly in regard to the provision of semi-sheltered or flexible employment for those with health problems. Again, the point to be made here is not that improvements in the working or retirement situation of affected workers are obvious or easily made but that the issue needs greater attention in policy relating to the employment circumstances of older workers who have poor health.

86

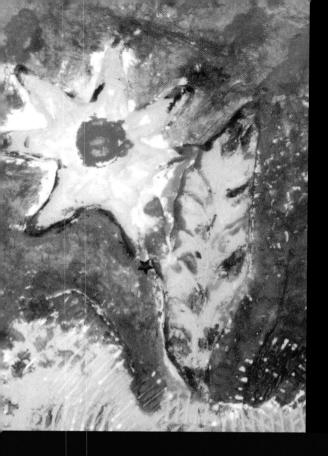

References

References

Barrett, A., Callan, T., Doris, A., O'Neill, D., Russell, H., Sweetman, O., & McBride, J. 2000, *How Unequal? Men and Women in the Irish Labour Market* Dublin: Oak Tree Press.

Costello, Ned., 2001. 'Training, Retraining and Lifelong Learning for Older Workers'. *In Conference Proceedings - Employment and Retirement among the Over 55s: Patterns, Preferences and Issues.* Dublin: National Council on Ageing and Older People.

Department of Social, Community and Family Affairs, 2001. *National Action Plan against Poverty and Social Exclusion 2001-2003.* Dublin: Stationery Office.

Department of Social Welfare, 1997. *'Supporting Voluntary Activity'* A Green Paper on the Community and Voluntary Sector and its Relationship with the State. Dublin: The Stationery Office.

Fahey, T., Russell, H., and Smyth, E. 2000, Gender Equality, Fertility Decline and Labour Market Patterns Among Women in Ireland, in *Bust to Boom?: The Irish Experience of Growth and Inequality*, B. Nolan, P. J. O'Connell, & C. T. Whelan, (eds.), Dublin: Institute of Public Administration, p. 244.

Fineman, S. (1983) *White Collar Unemployment: Impact and Stress*, Chichester: John Wiley & Sons

Fitzgerald, E., (2001) 'The Role of Pensions in the Decision to Retire from Paid Employment'. *In Conference Proceedings - Employment and Retirement among the Over 55s: Patterns, Preferences and Issues.* Dublin: National Council on Ageing and Older People

Garavan, R., Winder, R. and McGee, H., 2001. *Health and Social Services for Older People (HeSSOP).* Dublin: National Council on Ageing and Older People.

Ginn, J. & Arber, S. 1998, 'Pension Penalties: The Gendered Division of Occupational Welfare', *Work, Employment and Society*, vol. 7, no. 1, pp. 47-70.

Harney, M.(2000) *'Let Over 55s Contribute to the Boom'* Irish Times 19/7/2000

Hutch, M., 2001. 'Pensions Policy: Maintaining Established Living Standards in Older Age'. *In Conference Proceedings - Towards a Society for All Ages.* Dublin: National Council on Ageing and Older People.

Jahoda, M. (1982) *Employment and Unemployment: A Social-Psychological Analysis*, Cambridge: Cambridge University Press.

Layte, R., Fahey, T., and Whelan, C. T. 1999, *Income Deprivation and Well-Being Among Older Irish People.* Dublin: National Council on Ageing and Older People.

Lorence, J. (1987) 'Age Differences in Work Involvement: Analyses of Three Explanations', *Work and Occupations*, Vol. 14.

Loscocco, K. A. and Kalleberg, A. L. (1988) 'Age and the Meaning of Work in the United States and Japan', *Social Forces*, Vol. 67, No. 2, pp337-356.

Loftus, M., 2001. 'Chairperson's Address'. *In Conference Proceedings-Towards a Society for All Ages.* Dublin: National Council on Ageing and Older People

Mangan, I., 2001. 'Older People's Access to Work, Education, Training and Information Technology: Issues for Policy'. *In Conference Proceedings-Towards a Society for All Ages.* Dublin: National Council on Ageing and Older People.

O'Connor, P. 1998, *Emerging Voices: Women in Contemporary Irish Society.* Dublin: Institute of Public Administration.

Pahl, R. (1984) *Divisions of Labour*, Oxford: Basil Blackwell.

Russell, H. (1997) *Women's Experience of Unemployment: A study of British Women in the 1980s'* D.Phil. Thesis, University of Oxford.

Russell, H. 1998, "The Rewards of Work," in *British and European Social Attitudes the 15th Report: How Britain Differs*, R. Jowell *et al.*, (eds.), Aldershot: Ashgate.

Russell, H. 2000, 'Frustrated Housewives or Unemployed Workers? the Case of Domestic Returners' in J. Darke, Ledwith,S.; Woods,R. (eds), *Women and the City: Visibility and Voice in Urban Space*, Hampshire: Palgrave.

Walby, S. (1986) *Patriarchy at Work: Patriarchal and Capitalist Relations in Employment*, Cambridge: Polity Press.

Warr, P. (1987) *Work, Unemployment and Mental Health*, Oxford: Oxford University Press.

Warr, P. & Payne, R. (1983) 'Social Class and Reported Changes in Behaviour after Job Loss' *Journal of Applied Social Psychology*, Vol. 13, 206-366.

Whelan, C.T. and Whelan, B.J. (1988). *The Transition to Retirement.* General Research Series No. 138. Dublin: Economic and Social Research Institute.

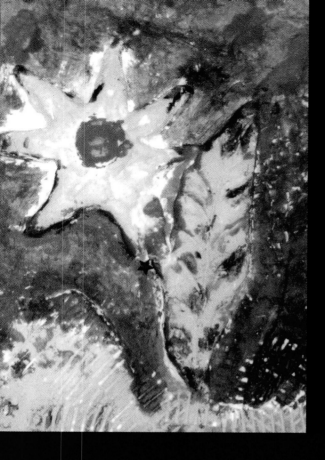

Terms of
Reference
and Membership

89

Terms of Reference

The National Council on Ageing and Older People was established on 19 March 1997 in succession to the National Council for the Elderly (January 1990 to March 1997) and the National Council for the Aged (June 1981 to January 1990).

The functions of the Council are as follows:

1. To advise the Minster for Health on all aspects of ageing and the welfare of older people, either at its own initiative or at the request of the Minister and in particular on:

    (a) measures to promote the health of older people;

    (b) measures to promote the social inclusion of older people;

    (c) the implementation of the recommendations contained in policy reports commissioned by the Minister for Health;

    (d) methods of ensuring co-ordination between public bodies at national and local level in the planning and provision of services for older people;

    (e) methods of encouraging greater partnership between statutory and voluntary bodies in providing services for older people;

    (f) meeting the needs of the most vulnerable older people;

    (g) means of encouraging positive attitudes to life after 65 years and the process of ageing;

    (h) means of encouraging greater participation by older people;

    (i) whatever action, based on research, is required to plan and develop services for older people.

2. To assist the development of national and regional policies and strategies designed to produce health gain and social gain for older people by:

   a) undertaking research on the lifestyle and the needs of older people in Ireland;

   b) identifying and promoting models of good practice in the care of older people and service delivery to them;

   c) providing information and advice based on research findings to those involved in the development and/or implementation of policies and services pertaining to the health, well-being and autonomy of older people;

   d) liaising with statutory, voluntary and professional bodies involved in the development and/or implementation of national and regional policies which have as their object health gain or social gain for older people.

3. To promote the health, welfare and autonomy of older people.

4. To promote a better understanding of ageing and older people in Ireland.

5. To liaise with international bodies which have functions similar to the functions of the Council.

The Council may also advise other Ministers, at their request, on aspects of ageing and the welfare of older people which are within the functions of the Council.

Membership

Chairperson Dr Michael Loftus

John Brady	Eamonn Kane
Noel Byrne	Patricia Lane
Kit Carolan	Dr Ruth Loane
Janet Convery	Leonie Lunny
John Cooney	Mary McDermott
Jim Cousins	Sylvia Meehan
Paul Cunningham	Dr Diarmuid McLoughlin
Joseph Dooley	Mary Nally
Iarla Duffy	Paddy O'Brien
James Flanagan	Pat O'Leary
Dr John Gibbon	Mary O'Neill
Prof Faith Gibson	Martina Queally
Frank Goodwin	Bernard Thompson
Dr Davida De La Harpe	Peter Sands
John Grant	

Director Bob Carroll